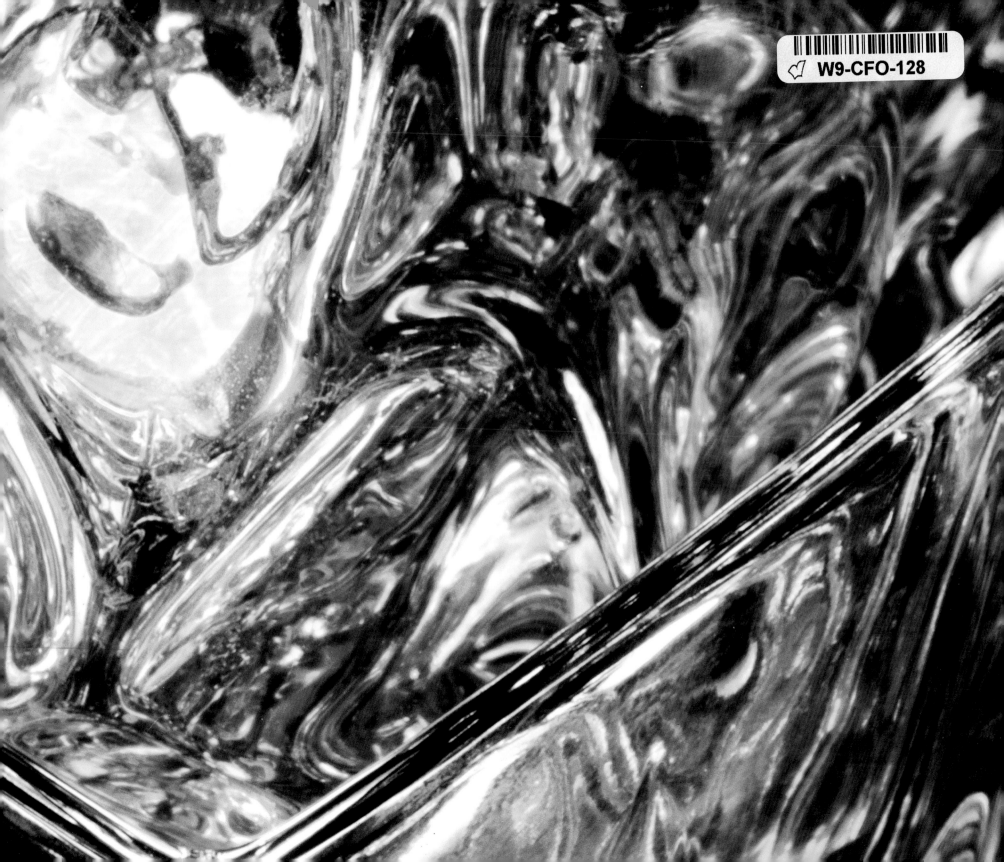

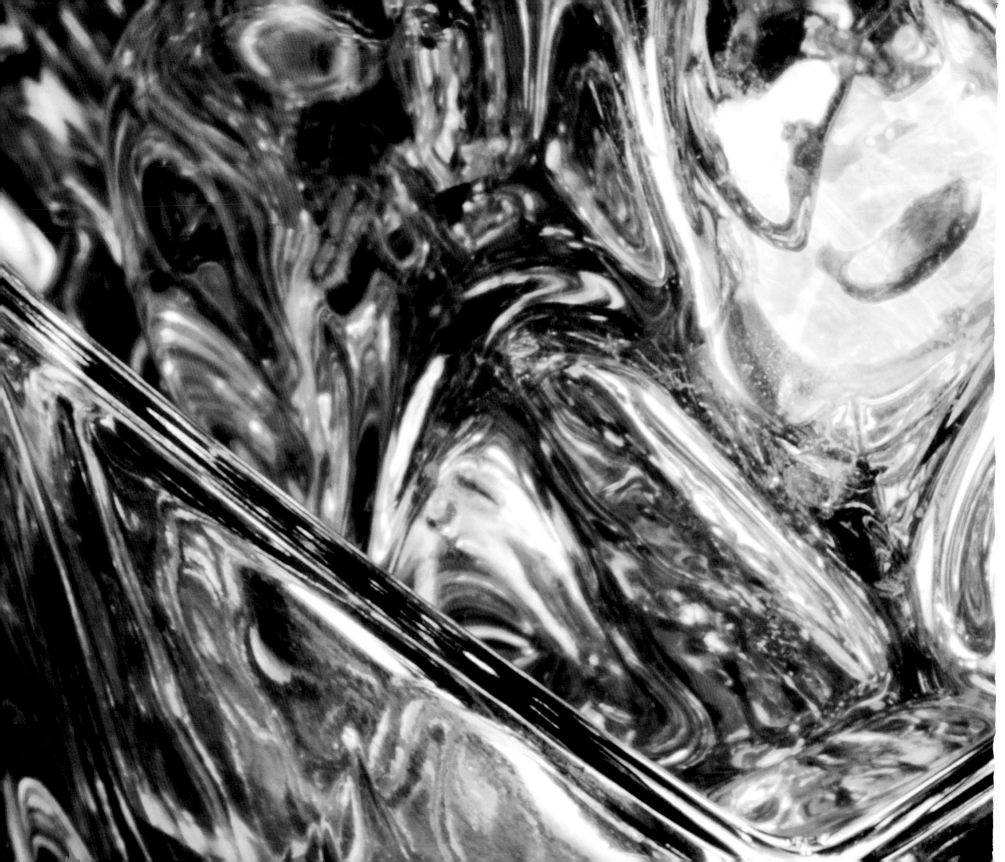

THE WOODFORD RESERVE®
CULINARY COCKTAIL TOUR

A JOURNEY WITH BOURBON

CONTENTS

FOREWARD

WOODFORD RESERVE'S CULINARY COCKTAIL TOUR: A JOURNEY WITH BOURBON seems to me more like a Woodford Reserve culinary scrapbook than a cookbook, as it catalogs our fondest guest memories, along with food, bourbon and cocktail discoveries. Friends, chefs, employees, guests and I have put together what may be the first-ever serious bourbon cookbook.

My love and passion for both place and product resulted in experimenting with Woodford Reserve and many food categories. We became maniacs for flavor. To anyone who questioned the real advantage of cooking and food pairings with Woodford Reserve, we immediately would say – "Taste it." As you'll see in the chefs' quotes, many epiphanies were unlocked. We even began dipping our chocolate chip cookies in Woodford Reserve!

You will see that most of our experimenting continued from the kitchen to the bar as we began treating bartenders as "Bar Chefs," taking our flavor wheel and applying the flavors to mixology and sensational cocktails.

Born and raised in the Bluegrass, I celebrate our local chefs, producers, the beauty of one of the oldest working distilleries and above all, my sincere desire to shout from the tallest mountain – "Kentucky has incredible culinary talent!" Many tourists have come to appreciate Woodford Reserve and the culinary events and offerings at the distillery. We invite whoever reads this book to come and visit the place that makes the finest, hand-crafted, premium bourbon in the world. Let us share with you a sip and taste of how 200 years of Kentucky bourbon-making and gracious southern cooking have blessed the Bluegrass!

To my favorite career, my Woodford Reserve family and friends

Peggy Stevens
Director, Homeplace Marketing
Master Taster

BOURBON REBORN: WOODFORD RESERVE'S FLAVOR WHEEL

Since the time Daniel Boone blazed the Wilderness Trail through a verdant Indian hunting ground known as Kentucky, whiskey has been used to enhance the flavors of food. The reason for this practice has never been explained or even advocated, really, but bourbon has been a part of time-honored Kentucky recipes for well over 200 years. Why is this? Well, Master Bourbon Taster Peggy Stevens and her team of Woodford Reserve Culinary Professionals set about finding out, and their discoveries were fascinating and conclusive.

To begin this culinary odyssey, Peggy and the Woodford Reserve Master Distiller took a panel of well-known regional chefs, and food and wine consultants through a thorough and extensive tasting of Woodford Reserve. Next came the pairing of Woodford Reserve with foods from seven basic flavor groups: bitter, sweet, tart, fruit, savory, herb and spice, and umami. Discoveries were made, blind notes were taken and suggestions were made to enhance the elements of each basic flavor group. At the end of the day, notes were compared and amazingly, this divergent group had reached a conclusion. Woodford Reserve is a versatile and wonderful enhancement to the flavor of food. Depending on its use, the result can be as noble as a French horn or as subtle as a cool, summer breeze. In order to clarify these findings, the Woodford Reserve Culinary Flavor Wheel was born.

The information contained in the Woodford Reserve Culinary Flavor Wheel is essentially simple stuff. The Woodford Reserve Culinary Professionals have suggested pairings with different foods and have offered suggestions for finished dishes fitting into each category. The classic and subtle nuances found in Woodford Reserve can be used to both enhance and alter basic food and cocktail flavors. For instance, the spice elements of Woodford Reserve can broaden the taste of pepper and cinnamon and takes on a new dimension when used in conjunction with this fine bourbon. Woodford Reserve used in basic vinaigrette can make the startling, bitter flavor of a radicchio salad sing. The heretofore under-analyzed flavors of the earth, found in mushrooms, truffles and certain milk products are redefined and reborn with the addition of Woodford Reserve.

Using the Woodford Reserve Culinary Flavor Wheel as a guide, some of the world's finest and most innovative chefs and bartenders are coming up with amazing new food pairings and flavor combinations. These talented men and women have certainly welcomed the coming of a new flavor foundation and they are taking the basics of the Woodford Reserve Culinary Flavor Wheel to wonderful new heights in the gastronomic world.

David Larson
Chef in Residence
The Woodford Reserve Distillery

INTRODUCTION

For centuries great cooks, particularly those from the Kentucky region, have known that fine food and fine bourbon are an inspired coupling. What's Derby brunch without mint juleps? Who would serve sacred slivers of perfectly aged country ham on beaten biscuits without a taste of perfectly aged bourbon on the side? And what is the only ingredient that could make iconic desserts such as bread pudding

and pecan pie even more delicious?

In the last decade, however, a new generation of cooks–regionally rooted, but not confined; blessed with remarkable locally grown and produced foodstuffs; and inspired by one of the finest bourbons ever distilled–have taken this tradition into surprising and utterly delectable new territory.

Consider the scallop, as Chef Ouita Michel of Holly Hill Inn in Midway, Kentucky, did. She then

expanded on its subtle sweetness with a fiery splash of bourbon to sear it in, and added a Woodford Reserve reduction that makes a very good thing extraordinary. Or stretch the imagination, as Chef Anthony Lamas of Louisville's Jicama Grill did, and dream up a pork tenderloin rubbed with rich and spicy adobo and then served up with a bourbon and chipotle-orange demi sauce that is nothing less than delectable.

Michel and Lamas are but two of the 12 regional chefs you will find

featured here who are exploring the qualities of Woodford Reserve–from subtle nuance to saporific zing–and creating a new and exciting culinary wave in the process. They were the grand prize winners in the Woodford Reserve Culinary Cocktail Tour of 2003, a headily delicious event that demonstrated palpably and palatably the versatility of this premium bourbon in the kitchen. Their recipes, as well as recipes from the Woodford Reserve Culinary Team, appear here.

Some of these recipes revisit classic territory with a new twist: chicken salad made with the bird poached in Woodford Reserve, its inherent sweetness enhanced by sweet cherries and nectarines; renowned Kentucky lamb, seasoned with spices and finished in a Woodford Reserve sweet and sour garlic syrup; southern hash dressed up with dried cherries and bourbon butter. Some of them feature a distinct foreign flair: penne pasta with chicken and mushrooms in a delectable bourbon alfredo;

Thai-inspired lettuce wraps with a Woodford Reserve-spiked peanut sauce. Many of them take advantage of the foodstuffs of the region: Woodford Reserve and sorghum syrup-marinated duck breast; bourbon-enhanced sweet potato puree; and pork medallions with fig and peach chutney.

You may think that what you hold in your hands is a cookbook full of delicious recipes and inventive suggestions for ways to use Kentucky's

finest premium bourbon. You would be right–but only partly so. The Woodford Reserve Cookbook is most definitely devoted to the art of fine food and beverage. In it you will find some 60 tantalizing, appetizing recipes that will not only please your taste buds, but will also introduce you to a remarkably versatile ingredient–one that will enhance the flavors coming out of your kitchen and spark your culinary imagination in fresh and genuinely exciting ways. In addition, you will also discover

classic and new cocktail recipes to enliven your entertaining. But in this book you will find much more than recipes. Here you will also find the story of a delightfully premium and versatile spirit, and the place and lifestyle from which it comes. And in the voices of the chefs, growers and food producers from that place, you will learn not only about the expanding culinary definition of fine Woodford Reserve bourbon, but about the growth and change in the traditions of American Southern cooking itself.

Revered southern cookbook author Marion Flexner, a Kentuckian herself, once commented that the ideal cookbook must contain a balanced blend of "fancibles" and "fillables." This book certainly does that. But in addition, it adds a new dimension to our understanding of American cooking by demonstrating the ability of bourbon, a purely American ingredient, to play a dramatic role in the contemporary

kitchen. Our chefs have discovered that bourbon has as much culinary versatility as wine and, in many cases, weighs in with even more resonance and wider nuance. It's their mission—and ours—to introduce you to the possibilities that Woodford Reserve can bring to your kitchen with this selection of contemporary recipes.

It's also our hope that these recipes will inspire you to create new Woodford Reserve combinations

yourself. To that end, we have included a section on the Woodford Reserve Culinary Flavor Wheel, a concept developed by The Woodford Reserve Distillery's Peggy Stevens to showcase Woodford Reserve's versatility as a flavor enhancer, and to suggest some truly inspired pairings.

Woodford Reserve is more than a simple whiskey. It is, in fact, an invitation to savor the gracious and hospitable lifestyle of a distinctive American culinary region.

John Egerton, author of Southern Food, a volume that serves as the Bible of its subject, describes Kentucky as a place where "glorious repasts have been a thriving tradition for more than two hundred years. No southern state except Louisiana has a more vibrant and ongoing food history than the Bluegrass state; its cookbooks, famous cooks, distinctive dishes and culinary lore combine to make a rich heritage that Kentuckians proudly claim as their own."

We note that Egerton describes the Kentucky tradition as "thriving," not past, and with this book we intend to celebrate not only the roots of food and hospitality in the Bluegrass region, but also the new growth of its continued creativity and discovery.

It's impossible to explore the subject of great bourbon without limning the place that gave birth to it—the fabled Bluegrass area of Kentucky—and the lifestyle of the region. We invite you to do that with

us in the next section, A Matter of Place and Time. Our Woodford Reserve Distillery sits in a region known for its tradition of gentle living, a place with time enough for porch sitting, thoroughbred raising, book reading, music making and bourbon sipping. The Woodford Reserve Distillery is a place where the hospitality is unsurpassed, the table filled with viands prepared with thoughtful care and bursting with the fresh harvested flavors of the

region. That table is most often ringed by the joyful faces of friends, old and new, gathered to celebrate nothing less than life itself. This is a place connected to the earth through its food and drink, which have in turn shaped the culture and lifestyle of the people who have consumed them. This is a place unlike any other and with this book we intend to welcome you to it, to The Woodford Reserve Distillery.

A MATTER OF PLACE & TIME

It was Kentucky poet and philosopher Wendell Berry who observed that in order to know who you are you must first know where you are. That profound connection to a sense of place characterizes virtually all great art of the southern United States. You can find it in the prose of Eudora Welty and the poetry of Billy Collins. You can see it in the art and the folk visions of Marvin Finn. You can hear it in a symphony of sound ranging from Stephen Foster to Bill Monroe to Howling Wolf to the B52s. And you can taste it in a sip of Woodford Reserve.

Yes, there is a metaphorical

for me what the piece of cake did for Proust."

But Woodford Reserve's connection to place is literal as well. By its very definition, bourbon is known by place. By law, only whiskey distilled in the United States may be designated bourbon. By tradition, the finest bourbons have long been deemed to come from the heart of Kentucky.

There is more than territorial hubris involved in the fact that more than 95% of the world's bourbon comes from Kentucky and in the connoisseur's belief that the best bourbon is produced in the state's Bluegrass region. Take a close look at the resources of this specific area and you may decide that

The Woodford Reserve Distillery, where bourbon has been made since 1812, Elijah Pepper chose this site for its ideal distilling attributes.

You may already know that many horse-fanciers believe it's the calcium in the water that makes the Bluegrass one of the greatest breeding grounds in the world for uncommonly swift and strong-boned thoroughbred horses. This same calcium reacts beautifully with the yeast used in the process of distillation, creating a whiskey that comes naturally to its potency and flavor. There are no artificial anythings added to Woodford Reserve. Our bourbon is the product of quality ingredients from the region interacting naturally.

Of those early settlers, most were of Scotch or Irish descent and many had been raised in the excellent whiskey making traditions of those countries. They may have thought at first that it was a cruel joke for nature to provide two of the finest resources for whiskey making without providing the grains they were accustomed to using for the mash for distilling. Undeterred, they made use of what was at hand, the native corn. And what began as an act of necessity turned into one of the most inspired inventions of the New World. Corn is a grain of perfect sweetness and subtlety. When distilled with great attention and patience, it makes a whiskey with depth and nuance

element in that last statement. The sweet molasses undertones, oaken resonance, and grassy freshness of a fine bourbon such as Woodford Reserve can conjure up immediately the image of a wide veranda looking out on an undulating wave of Bluegrass hills speckled with fleet-footed ponies. Close your eyes and you may imagine the sounds of cardinals in the dogwood and redbud trees, the soft clink of old silver being laid on a white-clothed table filled with savory two-year-old country ham, steaming spoonbread, fresh tomatoes and berries, and bacon-simmered green beans. As southern author Walker Percy once said, "Bourbon does

Mother Nature had sipping whiskey in mind all along when she invented Kentucky.

Start with the water, the most fundamental ingredient in the distillation of any spirit. Early settlers to the region called the water here "sweetwater." That's because central Kentucky's aquifer is cradled in limestone. Flowing through this porous rock, the water is cleansed of any impurities, such as iron, that might mar its flavor straight, or the velvety sensation of bourbon distilled from it. At the same time that it is acting as a purifier, the natural limestone filter contributes magnesium and calcium.

Superb water was not the only resource the early distillers found in Kentucky. When this Native American hunting ground was settled by early Euro-American colonists in the 1700s, the region was covered in stands of mature oak. There are 17 varieties of oak native to Kentucky, including the white oak that is perfect for making the barrels essential to the fine whiskey aging process. Charred on the inside of the barrel, this clean, sweet wood contributes a flavor to the spirits that is so distinctive no barrel is used for maturing bourbon more than once. Wood for the barrels used to age Woodford Reserve still comes from white oak.

unmatched by any other. So it is, then, that even when other grains became readily available, corn predominated in the mash because of its outstanding qualities. Now any bourbon must, by law, contain at least 51% corn in its mash mix. In addition we use a mix of rye, which contributes spicy undertones, and the rest is malted barley, which adds to the cereal resonance. The corn we use still comes from the Central Kentucky region, naturally one of the finest places in the world for growing high quality field corn.

Is it any wonder that Kentuckians are sincerely proud of their state?

"If, beyond the pearly gates, I am

permitted to select my place at the table, it will be among Kentuckians," historian Thomas D. Clark has written. "Eating dinner in Kentucky is more than a physiological refueling of the human body. It is a joyous social ritual."

That ritual evolved in tandem with, and perhaps was influenced by, the ever-refining art of making great bourbon. Although the region was rough initially, and so was the young whiskey made here at first, time was a powerful mellowing factor for both. The sloping hills of the Bluegrass, the rich soil and rippling water soon tempered the rough and tumble pioneer spirit of the first settlers. Plenty of fire was left in the character of the people of this

region, but over time it was mellowed so that folks from the area became known equally for their wit and humor as for their warmth and hospitality. People in these parts discovered the value of time spent creatively and socially. The arts of storytelling, making music, working in community to raise a barn or put up a field of tobacco became characteristic of the region. And so did the arts of fine cooking and entertaining. From sumptuous suppers in the fine houses of the gentry to simple farm meals featuring a staggering array of fresh vegetables and farm-raised and cured meat, Kentuckians became known for the

lavish tables they spread and their eagerness to welcome friend and stranger to them. Time was not considered wasted if it was spent on the preparation of good food, or in the company of good friends—ideally accompanied with a glass of fine bourbon.

Likewise, early distillers discovered that time could be an improving factor for their product. (At Woodford Reserve time is honored even in the earliest stages of the whiskey-making process. Our sour mash ferments in cypress tanks throughout the week, contributing rich subtleties to the final product.) The early distillers soon realized that when allowed to work

over time, the barrels they were using for shipping their whiskey could contribute to the ultimate flavor, particularly when the inside was charred. As we've noted, this is a region of great storytelling and there's plenty of folklore about the origins of this practice of burning the inside of bourbon barrels. Food historian, author and celebrated Southern raconteur Eugene Walter liked to tell that it was a huge lightning strike—a literal act of divinity—that charred the inside of a stash of buried whiskey barrels. When the earthly maker of the brew dug them up a few years later, Walter loved to say, he discovered an

elixir so exquisite a new distilling tradition was born.

But it was at the site of The Woodford Reserve Distillery in the early 1800s that Dr. James Crow, master distiller, perfected the process. His fundamental systems for preparing the barrels are still carefully carried out today for Woodford Reserve barrels. Our barrels are first toasted on the inside, caramelizing the natural sugars in the oak. Then they are charred to create a porous surface through which the distilled whiskey can pass, picking up color, vanilla flavors and countless subtleties from the caramelized layer of wood.

To gather the full nuance of

flavors that the oak proffers, the liquid in the barrel must pass in and out through this inside layer of wood repeatedly over a period of time. This process occurs as naturally as breathing when the barrels are stored in a climate with definite changes in temperature and humidity, such as the climate of central Kentucky. This process, repeated over time, turns pure new spirit into a heavenly drink. In fact, you can smell the process at work as you stand in the stone aging warehouses with two-foot thick walls next to Glenn's Creek at Woodford Reserve. The rows of wooden barrels stacked to the ceiling in these, the

oldest surviving stone aging warehouses in the Commonwealth, emit the distinctive fragrance of bourbon as it evaporates, and distillers have come to refer to the loss of volume through evaporation that is responsible for the delicious scent in the air as the "Angel's Share."

Bourbon must be taken from the barrel and bottled when the time is exactly right. Taken too soon, the liquid can be raw and fiery; allowed to sit too long, the bourbon can become woody and bitter. Getting the timing exactly right is an art of time and judicious consideration. At The Woodford Reserve Distillery, for example, the bourbon chosen to be bottled as Woodford Reserve is hand-selected by the master distiller. And it is this master distiller alone who determines when the time is ready.

Can it be that waiting for bourbon to age to perfection is a skill enhanced by a regional culture that has turned the act of waiting—also known as porch-sitting—into a fine art? Well, consider that for years the master distiller at Woodford Reserve was Lincoln Henderson, one of only three Americans invited each year to be a judge at the International Wine and Spirits Competition in London, England. Henderson was a man surely influenced by the traditions of his region, for his official biography says: "His idea of heaven involves a porch, a swing, a breeze, and a few fingers of Woodford Reserve Distiller's Select."

But perhaps the final words on time belong to yet another artist from this place, Kentucky-born, Atlanta-based food writer Reagan Walker, who has summed the art of bourbon-making up neatly: "Yes, time can be put in a bottle and it tastes smooth."

THE
WOODFORD
RESERVE
DISTILLERY

27

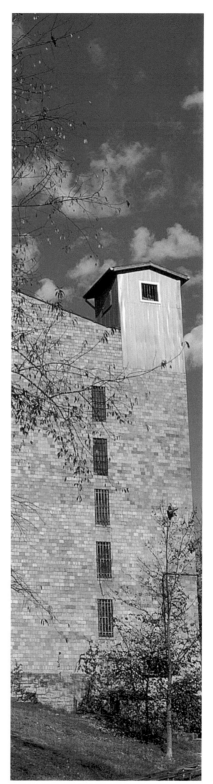

BARREL
WAREHOUSE

CIRCA 1934

FEATURED
CHEFS

PENG S. LOOI

Peng S. Looi has a degree in civil engineering. It's no surprise, then, that the new facility for Asiatique, the Pacific Rim restaurant he and his partner opened in the mid-1990s, is a fantastic structure. Built inside an overgrown brick bungalow on a busy commercial road, the restaurant leaves the bustle of the street and the limits of the house behind. Intimate dining rooms that spiral upward and levels have open interior windows to look out and down on the spaces below. It feels a bit like a Bauhaus tree house inside, one of perfectly layered proportions.

Those are apt words to describe the beautifully structured food that comes from Peng's kitchen, as well. The artful plates are often visual marvels of structure, and always a matter of perfectly layered flavors. They build on Peng's back-ground as a native of Malaysia (Chinese, Malay, Indian, and other Asian culinary influeces). "I learned to cook before I left home for England (he attended high school in Manchester) because I knew as a student that I couldn't eat out all the time and also that I'd get homesick" he says.

Home now is Louisville, Kentucky, where Peng moved to attend Speed Scientific School at the University of Louisville in the 1980s, earning that degree, but learning that he'd rather be building a repertoire in the kitchen. His first venture, August Moon, is still a popular fusion eatery with a passionate regular clientele. Asiatique is where he branches out in even more dramatic ways.

"My type of cooking has no borders," he says. Malaysia, he notes, "is a country of immigrants, just like America. You encounter all sorts of cultures and their food there. Fusion is what I grew up with." Cooking with spirits was part of the tradition he grew up with, too. "Chinese people do like to use brandy or fermented wine in cooking. You'll find saki, even champagne. I like scotch and I used scotch in England."

"Then here I discovered Woodford Reserve, which has that same nice oak-y, smoky, earthy aroma, but also some sweetness that makes it even more versatile. I like for my ingredients to pop", he says, eyes widening for emphasis. Bourbon accelerates the pop of any number of ingredients in Peng's kitchen, from espresso to lemon grass. And when it doesn't go in the dish itself, he's a great fan of the bourbon cocktail, or a light bourbon sorbet for after dinner.

PATRICK COLLEY

"I have 900 bosses," Patrick Colley says with a grin. As the executive chef at the venerable Louisville Country Club he is encouraged by those bosses/members to work in a traditional southern vernacular. And he notes that his own "comfort zone" is in modern southern food, having trained at Johnson and Wales in Charleston, South Carolina, where he then worked for many years, as well as in Dallas and Cape Cod, before returning to his hometown.

That said, "I try to be very broad in my definition of what southern food is. I want people to say, 'Mmmmm, what's that in there? What's that great taste about?' Bourbon can create that certain sense of something special; make people say, "I like that flavor! What is it?'"

Bourbon is virtually a tradition at this place, Patrick says. The subdued red club chairs in the lounge, the tall brown leather chairs at the bar, and the wide verandas looking out on rolling grassy lawns suggest a place where some serious sipping is in order. "Some clubs are scotch," he says, "but this is most definitely a good southern bourbon club."

Nevertheless, Patrick confesses that his initial culinary impression of bourbon was that it was primarily an ingredient for the dessert menu. "Then I had a little education prior to the Woodford Reserve Culinary Cocktail Tour. We were tasting the bourbon with a number of items and I was so surprised at the subtleties that are present in it because of the aging and distilling processes" he says. "I realized it was an ingredient that could enhance other flavors without overwhelming them. Now we make a lot of our meat sauces with Woodford. There's an affinity for vanilla, especially the vanilla bean, it goes so well in a more savory context, particularly with duck, veal and quail."

"Not all bourbons are so versatile in the kitchen. It can be dominant or minor in a recipe. Not only does Woodford add accents, but it takes on other flavors very well. It's not often that you find an ingredient that is both a good giver and receiver of flavors. I guess you could say it plays well with others," he says, and grins again.

NATHAN CARLSON

Nathan Carlson describes himself as "an avid outdoor kind of guy." Then he laughs and says, "You can build up quite an appetite outside. Maybe that's why I gravitated toward the kitchen."

By the age of 17, the Louisville native was working in restaurant kitchens full-time in a variety of jobs. It was in Chef Joe Castro's kitchen at the English Grille in the Brown Hotel that he began to get his bourbon education.

From there he went to Washington State to work, in part because of the outdoor scene

there, "but Kentucky just pulled on me. It's hard to leave here," he notes.

When the 30-year-old chef was invited to assume the head kitchen role at the newly opening Avalon in Louisville, he jumped at the chance. "I got to design the kitchen, knock out some walls from the restaurant that was here before, open up the place. I even got to work a little in the front of the house. I love working with space."

He calls the food at Avalon "Fresh American Cuisine" which means "we can do what we want to do to make the most of fresh and regional

ingredients." And what he wants to do quite often is to utilize the flavors of fine bourbon.

"I like Woodford Reserve, especially when there's something sweet in a recipe. That doesn't mean it doesn't go with a savory dish, but that it still accents the sweetness. I like to use it in a chutney or sauce. When it came time to create a recipe for the Culinary Cocktail Tour, I knew right away that I wanted it to go with a really good steak. Woodford has a caramel-ly, orangey, vanilla flavor that goes just great with a seared piece of excellent meat." Nathan compares bourbon to wine in another respect, noting that the variety of bourbons creates a broad taste spectrum. "If you're going to cook with it, you're going to have to taste what's out there to know how to use it. Ah, it's a terrible job," he says, and then laughs gleefully.

DEAN CORBETT & DAVE CUNTZ

There is a platter of bear bacon in the kitchen of Equus. "Is that a Kentucky thing," a visitor asks? Executive Chef Dave Cuntz grins and says, "Actually we get that from up north, Michigan I think."

"We're not a southern restaurant per se," he says. "We don't want to be restricted by labels, and our cooking style is more eclectic than that."

"What we are is ingredient-driven," notes chef/owner Dean Corbett. "And almost from the time we opened, those ingredients have been from around here." "Here" is the St.Matthews neighborhood of Louisville where the restaurant has been a bastion of fine drink and dining since 1985. Dean put out the word and almost immediately farmers began coming to the back door of his place with their best products, a tradition that continues today.

Not content, he also roams the local markets on his shiny chrome Harley-Davidson, a chef's toque on the gas tank. "One day I was driving past this church up the street and I caught these tomatoes and squashes out of the corner of my eye in the parking lot," Dean says. You can almost hear the squeal of the tires and see the dust kicked up as

he wheeled back around. "I started walking through these baskets of the most beautiful produce I'd ever seen, looking for a bag to fill. Then this nice guy comes up and says, 'Do you know what this is?'"

It was delivery day for Ewingsford Farm and the nice guy was Steve Smith, one of the first and finest CSAs in Kentucky. "I found out you couldn't buy the stuff outright; you had to be a member," Dean laughs. "But memberships are cheap, and the vegetables are so good. The restaurant might have to do that next year."

That emphasis on extreme quality is the key to an ingredient - driven restaurant, Dave notes. "We're always looking for the best product we can find, no matter the cost."

But bottom line, cost may prove to be less when the product is good. "Take premium bourbon," Dean says. The restaurant uses bourbon frequently in the kitchen. "We only use the best, and in the end, it's not more costly. If you're cooking with Woodford Reserve, you use so much less of it than if you're cooking with a cheaper, less complicated and mellow blend. If you use the cheap stuff up front, you have to doctor it with other ingredients; you have to cook it down to get it to mellow out. With Woodford, it's just a splash and you're there. Full of flavor."

JOHN CASTRO

Ask John Castro when he first encountered bourbon as a culinary ingredient and he won't miss a beat before replying , "Mother's milk." Ah,

the world of comedy may have lost a star when John decided to take up a spatula instead. Now he wields it as the executive chef of Winston's, the award winning restaurant at Sullivan University's National Center for Hospitality Studies in Louisville, where he is also an instructor.

A bit more seriously, John notes that his mother made a number of

desserts with bourbon, most memorably a black cherry gelatin with miniature marshmallows pinched in half and black walnuts throughout. "She got it from an old bourbon cookbook that her mother had back in Meade County."

"We also had a fabulous eggnog at our house with a bourbon spike that you start six months before. That's when you add one whole cracked nutmeg, two vanilla beans and three sticks of cinnamon to the bottle. Believe me, it adds to your holiday cheer."

John encountered fusion cooking right out of the cradle. Raised in southern Indiana, his mother brought the Kentucky traditions to the table while his father's background was Asian. Both parents cooked, as does John's brother, Joe, the executive chef at the English Grille in Louisville's Brown Hotel.

"And then you discover that you can change the character of the bourbon by how you choose to use it, and it becomes even more versatile" he notes. "If you cook it for a while, that will make it softer. If you want it to stand up and say 'hi,' you add it at the last, to say, the whipped cream."

More heavenly matches: bourbon mixed with sweet sorghum and vinegar for a great salad dressing for crisp greens and in almost anything Asian. "It's those caramel notes that make it really work with Asian."

John describes the distinctive taste of Woodford Reserve as "incredibly round. It releases on the palate with a bit of a sting, but a soft, well-rounded sting. It's capable of mixing with so many things."

"I was so excited when I saw the Flavor Wheel. It's such a great concept! I showed it to my students and they thought it was simply amazing!"

ANTHONY LAMAS
(Winning Recipe Louisville)

"You know, being from California, bourbon wasn't around that much," notes Anthony Lamas, executive chef/owner of the Jicama Grill in Louisville, Kentucky. "Rum was really the big influence in my cooking. But once I started cooking in Kentucky, I discovered that bourbon works much the same way, only with its own accent. I love the kind of caramel it brings on in anything it touches."

And diners love the layers of flavor Anthony brings to anything he touches as well. His restaurant regularly makes the top five lists of outstanding eateries in Kentucky's largest city–a dauntingly great restaurant town–and his work earned him a Rising Star chef dinner at the James Beard House in 2004.

To say the deft young chef is rooted in Latino tradition may be an understatement. His mother was from Mexico, his father from Puerto Rico, and by the time Anthony was five-years-old, he was already working in family-owned restaurants in L.A. That was followed by several years working in some of the best restaurants in southern California where he honed his skills as a creator of a distinctive Pacific Rim cuisine and melded it with the foodways he'd grown up with. "Nuevo Latino" is the name Anthony gives to this fusion cooking style–one rooted in his family traditions, but has no trouble translating in his new hometown in Kentucky.

In fact, local southern traditions and products have given another dimension to Anthony's oeuvre. His prize-winning adobo pork tenderloin comes served with a sweet corn grit cake spiked with chipotle, all of it laced together with a Woodford Reserve orange demi sauce.

With a world of ingredients to choose from, Anthony says that the bottom line for him is a product's inherent quality. "And in that respect," he notes, "you cannot do better than Woodford Reserve. It's no ordinary bourbon. It's like a wine. You don't use an inferior wine when you cook. And I love to cook with bourbon, so I'm going to use the one that brings the most complexity to the recipe."

It also apparently brings inspiration. Invited to cook a meal featuring bourbon at the James Beard House in late 2004, Anthony has dreamed up a savory bread pudding with apples, walnuts, foie gras, Maytag bleu cheese and Woodford Reserve. Then, mindful of the bourbon's sugar notes, he's going to use it to make a marinade with aji Amarillo chile that will season shrimp to be cooked and served on skewers made of sugar cane.

JIM GERHARDT & MICHAEL CUNHA

Even when he was being lavished with praise nationally as executive chef of the Oak Room in Louisville's legendary Seelbach Hotel, Jim Gerhardt's dream was to have his own restaurant, an up-scale casual place that showcased the outstanding products and traditions of Kentucky.

So when he and chef partner Michael Cunha brought that dream to life in 2003, they chose Limestone for the restaurant's name–the key to two of Kentucky's finest creations, thoroughbred horses and sublime bourbon.

"Visiting a distillery like Woodford Reserve is a remarkable benefit from being in this region," Jim says. "It not only broadens your understanding of how the bourbon is made, but also of how you can use it. For instance, you look at the mash

bill, and if it's finished with rye, the bourbon will be more savory. Then you know it's perfect for a cioppino or to stir into barley soup for a hearty, smoky finish."

Aging increases the bourbon's caramel and vanilla tones, he notes; but youth has its advantages as well. "Lately I've been working with new spirit. I got interested in how it tasted just off the still. It's comparable to a fine vodka or grappa. And it works in cooking as well; you can use it to good end instead of pepper!"

Many bourbons tend to fall squarely into the sweet or savory camp, but Jim notes that, "Woodford Reserve is an exception in that it works both ways. In cooking, as in most things, the key to excellence is balance. The master distiller does a remarkable job in evaluating the consistency and age, choosing the blend to create that balance in Woodford."

Consequently, the bourbon ends up in a plethora of dishes at Limestone. And if that's not enough, the restaurant uses staves from discarded aging barrels to smoke some of its ingredients– vegetables, fish, braised lamb shoulder–and as distinctive plates for serving certain specialties.

BRIAN JENNINGS

When Brian Jennings was fourteen years old, he read an article in the Smithsonian *magazine about chefs in America.* "It sounded good to me."

Already he had a grounding in things culinary. "I grew up in Minneapolis and my grandmother was second-generation Polish. She was a wonderful cook of all those European specialties. She would cook for six to eight people a day, and then friends would drop by. She was a whirlwind of a cook. She liked to experiment with the new recipes of the day, too."

And she let her grandson cook with her. "I was something of a casual participant. There was a garden full of fresh produce in the back yard and I'd get sent out to get things from it. I got to help making a few dishes, like pierogies, and the homemade kraut. You want to talk about a hands-on cooking experience; you just put your hand into the sauerkraut barrel."

From kraut he moved on to the California Culinary Academy in San Francisco where he learned a great deal about technique, both classic and contemporary, and a lot about wines and food pairings. For 16 years he's been cooking with the Hyatt Regency firm, in Los Angeles, Austin, Chicago, New Mexico and now, for the last three years, in Lexington, Kentucky.

Brian has plunged into the food culture of Kentucky wholeheartedly. Local grits show up on the Hyatt menu with regularity, and much as his grandmother's garden supplied her kitchen, the Lexington farmer's market sets up right outside of the Hyatt twice a week, bringing produce from folks like Bill Best, the famous bean and tomato man from Berea, or fresh garlic from the folks at Blue Moon Farm, just down the road near Richmond.

"I try to liven the menu with the best foods I can find locally," he notes. "How could I not when the farmers are right outside the door? And when the folks show up who have an appreciation for fine wines, well that's when you bring out the bottle of Woodford Reserve for savoring."

NAT TATE

It was a circuitous route that led Nat Tate back home again to Lexington, Kentucky. First he headed east to the Culinary Institute in New York where he got a solid grounding in the skills and techniques of the kitchen. Then it was west for the young man, to the Napa Valley. That was an education, as well, in wines and in using abundant fresh and local products to make an impact on flavor.

"Yes, California is something like a culinary promised land," Nat says, but you can't keep a Kentucky boy–particularly a devoted Wildcats basketball fan–away from the homeplace too long. "I wanted to come back and the opportunity to work at Portofino seemed like the perfect one. It's an Italian restaurant with California flair, which means we have free range to be eclectic."

What surprised Nat when he returned was the blossoming of the local Kentucky food scene. "I was pleasantly surprised when I got here. The general restaurant boom that started in the 1980s is really going strong in both Lexington and Louisville. But even more surprising was the progress in the agricultural scene. I'm really proud of what Kentucky is producing now. We're right up there in the mix with some of the great food regions of the country. Food is such a part of our nature, our culture, and you can see that more and more in the restaurants that are using the products of the region and in the markets where things are being sold."

Just as he's adapted Napa concepts to local produce, Nat has also translated some California-style cooking with wine into bourbon-flavored cuisine. "Bourbon is a little more challenging than wine at first. You have to consider its properties," he notes. "Age can really make a difference. And often you will want to work with the bourbon, cook it, for instance, to reduce the sugar content. But once you get the knack, it's a fine ingredient, able to do many of the same things wine does from macerating fruit to deglazing a pan.

"And when you get a bourbon that starts with this clear, sweet limestone water of Kentucky–when you start that pure and you triple distill it, then you end up with such a smooth product, it would be a crime not to use it."

49

ROD JONES

It's not that Rod Jones has a thing against culinary school. "I think it's great for the kind of training it is. It exposes kids to a lot of terrific ideas. But when you come out of culinary school, what you're armed with is theory. When you come up through the ranks in actual restaurant kitchens, well, what you know, you really know it.

Rod came up through the ranks starting at the Coach House in Lexington where he worked both in the kitchen and as a musician. "Stanley Demos (the owner of the legendary eatery) heard me play and told me to give it up and be a cook. I think he was right."

Back again to Lexington, he opened the Atomic Café, a lively eatery devoted to Caribbean fusion. He's worked in an upscale deli, a fine Italian restaurant and the University of Kentucky faculty club. And now he feels he's found the place where all of these disparate adventures can come together in a dynamite menu, Rossi's. The café and nightspot has been a fixture near the University for the last four years, but has recently moved to a new facility featuring lots of blond wood and a very contemporary atmosphere. "That's our food, too: contemporary and bright."

Rod has worked with a variety of spirits in the kitchen including Irish whiskey. And then he had a bourbon epiphany. "Bourbon has more sugar, more nose than an Irish whiskey, and that makes it more adaptable. I didn't realize though, that you could sit down and drink it with a meal, just like a fine wine," he says.

One of Rod's favorite creations is a cocktail with Woodford Reserve, blackberries, peaches and some simple syrup. "I think it's better than sangria."

And in the kitchen? "Once I understood how a really fine Woodford Reserve bourbon could go with any-thing–even a great piece of cheese–there was no end to it," he notes. "Here in Kentucky, you know, you can put bourbon on anything."

OUITA MICHEL
(Winning Recipe Lexington)

Ouita Michel didn't aim to be a new Kentucky chef. "I meant to be a lawyer," she says, describing her intentions when she left her home state for New York. Well, you know what they say about intentions. Instead she found herself cooking in the restaurants of the big city and loving it.

"I did macrobiotics in one place, then seafood in another. The sheer diversity of it was wonderful," she said. Law school ambitions were soon replaced by enrollment at the CIA, where she met her husband, Chris, and graduated as class valedictorian. When the couple came back to Kentucky to get married in 1993, Ouita says she had no intentions of remaining: "But when I got here, I found I just couldn't leave. I realized I wanted to cook for my friends and my family. I realized that I missed community."

Community is certainly what she and Chris have created around the restaurant at Holly Hill Inn, a lovely 150-year-old Midway, Kentucky, house on the National Register of Historic Places. The menu there pays more than lip service to the concept of regional cooking. "In the summer 80% of what we use in the kitchen comes from the region, mostly from Woodford County growers," Ouita says. Not surprisingly, That includes heirloom tomatoes, greens, haricot verts and tiny, scrumptious potatoes. It also includes lamb, chicken, eggs and grass-fed beef, organic asparagus, local honey, grits from nearby Weisenberger Mill and more. Even the flowers on the tables come from local growers.

Using such local bounty in recipes that are rooted in southern tradition but bound only by her imagination, Ouita has earned national accolades, including a coveted Beard nomination for outstanding chef in her region. But it's still the local community that holds her heart.

It's natural, then, that Ouita would gravitate to the bourbon that is made just up the road from her kitchen. "I started using bourbon in desserts when I worked in Lexington," she said. But when she started her own place, she decided to branch out.

"You have to get over the chocolate and pork hump," she said, noting the two most common culinary pairings for bourbon. Her epiphany came when Peggy Stevens did a tasting of foods with Woodford Reserve. "What really struck me was how fantastic it was just served with slivers of Pecorino," she says. "I kept finding new dimensions in both the bourbon and the cheese. It got me seriously thinking about the undertones of Woodford Reserve and how they could be utilized."

CRAIG THOMPSON
(former chef of Harper's Restaurant)

The fact that Craig Thompson came up with a prize-winning recipe using Woodford Reserve has a hint of fate about it.

Craig grew up in Wisconsin, trained at the California Culinary Academy and cooked in wine country. From there he went to Vail for five years, then Hilton Head, South Carolina, before taking the head chef position at Harper's Restaurant in Louisville, Kentucky.

You could say Craig got an immersion course in ritual southern cooking, arriving as he did one week before the Derby. "It was a great way to get introduced to the traditions of the region," he said with a grin. "At Derby time it's everything southern and everything Kentucky and I felt like I was in the advanced class in local cooking. I have an affinity for working with the flavor of places, particularly distinctive local ingredients. In San Francisco that meant cooking with wine, in Colorado, the local beers. In Kentucky that means bourbon."

To discover more about the region's finest potable, Thompson took his visiting parents on a tour of the Bluegrass region. A little sheepishly, he admits that they were actually on their way to another distillery. "I had just moved here myself and I went to the visitor's center and got directions to another place where they make bourbon. The thing is, I'm not a very good navigator, but you might say I'm a lucky one. Instead of getting where I

was headed, we ended up following the signs on I-64 that led us to the distillery and an education in Woodford Reserve. I can tell you that it has had a real impact on my cooking ever since."

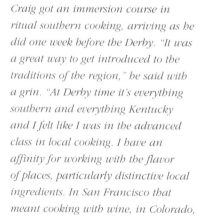

Like most California-trained chefs, Thompson is well versed in the use of a variety of wines in the kitchen. "Wine is great," he says. "It adds dimension to a dish. But bourbon is even better."

The reason is straightforward, he says: "Good bourbon has more character than even the best wines. The flavor is fuller, rounder and it holds up better in cooking. With wine, you inevitably lose aromatics when cooking. With bourbon, the opposite happens; the subtle flavors become more emphasized as the alcohol cooks down."

"I have worked with a number of bourbons, but what amazes me is how well the Woodford plays in a range of recipes, from desserts to very pungent appetizers."

TALENTED
PRODUCERS

BLUE MOON GARLIC

The voice of Van Morrison wafts from the old tobacco barn where Leo and Jean Pitches Keene are harvesting

a new crop of garlic. "She's as sweet as Tupelo Honey…" he croons, but the scent that fills the air is, in fact, pungent, nutty, tart and heady. The Keenes raise some 25 varieties of the essential herb: Chinese Pink, Oregon Blue, Killarney Red and Silverskin among them. They sell out their entire crop every year at Lexington and Louisville farmer's markets and to the mail-order customers who write in from around the country, a few from around the world.

Two things seem to make Blue Moon garlic special. First, there is the serious attention the Keenes pay to the details of every aspect of the herb, from lore and cooking tips to the best means of cultivation. Such passion has caused Leo and Jean to dub themselves and their most devoted customers "garlic-heads." The Keenes use garlic more than generously in their kitchen, Jean once concocting potato salad with 25 cloves in it. "I don't know what we'd do if we didn't grow garlic. We couldn't afford to buy it," she says.

But if you do, you won't have that second element that contributes to the particularly delicious flavors of Blue Moon's crop, the sweet bottom soil along the Kentucky River. The farm sits above a bend in the waterway in Madison County. The land is full of nutrients that Leo and Jean only add to using natural methods and ingredients. They use a crab and shrimp fertilizer that comes from Louisiana, sometimes traveling down to Bayou country to pick it up and take a rare break to frolic on the beach with their dogs, Luna Blue and Echo. (Their cat is named Machashi, after a favorite variety of the pungent bulb.) They use no petro-chemical fertilizers, herbicides nor pesticides, Blue Moon was certified organic for many years, but when the paperwork for certification became overwhelming, the Keenes decided, as many small organic farmers have lately, to simply say their crop is "sustainably grown" and explain to new customers what that means. Their tried and true community of garlic-heads knows that what they purchase from Blue Moon is pure garlic goodness, and nothing more.

BILL BEST

Summer Saturday mornings–there may be folks sleeping late in Lexington, but not anyone who loves great food. Instead they are gathered at the farmer's market, waiting for Bill Best's

truck to arrive, loaded with heirloom tomatoes and green beans.

Anna Russians, Yellow Germans, Kentucky Beefsteak–the names of the old variety tomatoes Bill grows delight the tongue almost as much as their bright, intense flavors do. Restaurateurs vie with connoisseurs for the most unusual or beloved of the 150 varieties he raises each year. The beans have charming monikers, too: Tobacco Worm, Lazy Wife, Fat Man, and Rogue Mountain, for the small peak that rises next to the Best's farm in Berea, Kentucky.

Bill, a retired administrator from Berea College, has been a grower all of his life, helping his mother and grandmother in the gardens they nurtured in Western North Carolina, where he was born. It was his vivid memory of the flavors from the produce of those days that started him on the path of heritage and heirloom seed-saving.

The taste of the tomatoes he was growing from catalog seed just didn't measure up to those memories, so Bill began to search out the older varieties. A charter member of the Lexington farmer's market since 1972, and Berea's since 1973, he quickly discovered he wasn't the only man with a passion for flavor. Now his tomatoes sell by the truckload.

And so do his green beans. Meaty, succulent pods filled with beans and bursting with flavor, these are beans grown from seed that Bill has collected from Appalachian farmers in recent years. He has catalogued nearly 200 varieties with distinct variations in a personal seed bank that he distributes to other interested growers for a small fee. The Sustainable Mountain Agriculture Project has grown from those seeds to an organization devoted to finding ways to keep mountain farms alive and thriving. For his work, Bill was honored in 2003 with the Ruth Fertel Keeper of the Flame Award, presented by the Southern Foodways Alliance, and his produce is honored nightly in the fine restaurants of the region.

JOHN MEDLEY

When the folks at Churchill Downs decided to focus on regional products in food service for the 2004 Kentucky Derby, provisioning seemed a daunting

task. Where would they get 12,000 pounds of prime pork, for example, and in a matter of days.

Enter John Medley of Kentucky Heritage Meats. Medley's family has been raising hogs at Happy Hollow Farms in Washington County for three generations. Four years ago John decided to change the methods to a more natural routine. "I started talking to the people who were cooking the meat, and I discovered that there was a real demand for pork that was raised more naturally,"

Instead John decided to take his pork directly to the retail market. He began by selling at the Jeffersontown Farm's Market, outside of Louisville, and the quality of the meat was such that he soon attracted a market among local restaurateurs, In fact, sales were so good that John created a co-op among other like-minded hog producers in the region and opened a retail store. Now, nine producers provide pork and pork products,

including Happy Hollow's homemade sausage, John's country hams and country bacon, to the storefront and on-line store. Kentucky Home Grown Beef provides gorgeously marbled all-natural beef and the store also sells delicious Kentucky lamb from three farms in the region.

Pulling together the co-op and starting a retail market has been a difficult process. "It's like any new venture in that it takes time and it has its glitches," John says. It took a while to convince all of the other farmers to join him, for instance. "They wanted to wait a bit and see how it worked for me. I don't blame them. I'd have done the same. But then they saw there was a market for quality and that's all it took."

As for that Derby time order: Even though Kentucky Heritage Meats had only been open a couple of days, John was able to fill that six-ton request with all natural Kentucky-raised pork from the co-op within 24-hours. Now that's a winner!

JUDY SCHAD

The French term "terroir" is used to describe a group of vineyards from the same region and it indicates that the shared climate, soil, grapes and traditions of wine-making of that region contribute to the personality of the particular wines that are made there.

"I used to wonder if that concept was real, or more an affectation. But now I know it's real with all my heart," says Judy Schad. She and her husband, Larry, own Capriole Dairy just outside of Louisville, Kentucky. The fresh, ripened and aged chevre she makes there has won countless awards and is recognized as among the finest in North America.

"What I understand now," Judy says, "Is that the place reflects in everything you do. Once you root in a place, you become a part of its geography, and it affects everything you do. I mean the herd here is eating sumac and sassafras, because that's what's growing and has always grown here. And that is reflected in the milk."

She goes on to note that her cheese is further affected by the fact that the hilly and heavily forested region, while suited perfectly to goats, is less amenable to the pasture-oriented cow, so she's never had the option of using other types of milk to make her cheese. "And the climate here becomes a major factor in the types of cheese we make, even the limitations of our particular piece of land have an impact. We have learned, through trial and error, that we can't have a herd of much more than 450 goats, and that means we need to keep our production small and focused."

Place has had another impact on Capriole's production. "This place has provided a remarkable market. The restaurants in this part of Kentucky are truly extraordinary," she notes. "I was lucky. I could have been 20 minutes outside of almost any other medium-sized city in America and that would have been a sad story."

Instead, Capriole cheese appears regularly on the tables of the many great restaurants in Louisville, Lexington and the surrounding region, contributing to what might be called the "terroir" of the contemporary cuisine of Kentucky.

And from other producers of fine local product as well. "We just won three first prizes from the American Cheese Society for 2004," Judy says. "And two of the three featured Woodford Reserve. The first was a truly decadent chocolate and bourbon cheese torte, and the other was our classic Bannon, wrapped in chestnut leaves soaked in Woodford Reserve. You see? It all comes down to place."

PHILIP WEISENBERGER

The same corn that inspired Kentucky's distillers to reach for glory is the grain at the heart of the region's staff of life, cornbread. And if you think folks don't feel passionately about the homely pone, just try serving it to a true Kentuckian with sugar in it.

The cornmeal most preferred in the region is made from white corn and true aficionados like theirs stone-ground. Folks will go to great lengths to get just the right meal and that may explain why Weisenberger Mill has been grinding and selling white cornmeal, soft wheat flour and other products for nearly a century and a half.

The Weisenberger family bought the already operating mill on the South Elkhorn River in 1865, and has run it using water for stone and burr grinding for six generations since. Phil Weisenberger is retired, but comes in most everyday. His son, Mac, operates the mill with the help of his son, Philip. Other members of the family are on the small work crew as well. The plain three-story gray block building is itself on the National Register of Historic Places and there are old mill-

stones set into the stone walls that surround it.

But while the mill follows traditional methods–each bag of meal, flour or grits is filled by hand–the company has survived in part because the family has been willing to adapt to market demand. The Weisenbergers today sell some 70 products, including a breading mix for frying fish that local casters swear by. It's the cornmeal and the grits that regional restaurateurs love.

"I can't believe how lucky I am that the best grits in America come from the mill about five miles up the road," says chef Ouita Michel of Holly Hill Inn in nearby Midway, Kentucky.

WOODFORD
RESERVE
COCKTAILS

Chris Morris
Master Distiller

ABOUT WOODFORD RESERVE

It's true that while remarkable bourbon comes from Kentucky, not all Kentucky bourbons are equally remarkable. There are reasons why we believe that Woodford Reserve is the finest of all bourbons, and also why it lends itself exceptionally well to use as a culinary ingredient.

Woodford Reserve is a small batch bourbon. There are only ten bourbon distilleries in Kentucky and The Woodford Reserve Distillery is the oldest, smallest and slowest working distillery in the state.

Woodford Reserve's high-rye sour mash ferments for up to seven days in small cypress vats. This extra time allows the proprietary yeast to develop a broader complexity of flavors from the start. At this point, the mash becomes a "distiller's beer" and is ready for distillation.

From the vats, the beer flows to our small, distinctive distilling room dominated by three glowing copper pot stills imported from Scotland, the only ones like them in the United States. While their burnished beauty would be enough to commend them, these pot stills are not used solely for their appearance, but because we have determined that they do the job of distilling best. At Woodford Reserve, the distiller's beer that will become Woodford Reserve is triple-distilled, and the spirit safe in the still house allows the master distiller to watch its progress, determining when it is exactly right.

When that time comes, the distillate is transferred to hand-crafted new white oak barrels toasted and charred to our unique specifications. Only 70-105 barrels are filled each week at Woodford Reserve. That's all right. What we are after with Woodford Reserve is quality, not quantity.

Quality takes time. Our whiskey ages between six to eight years, which create a perfect micro-climate to facilitate the "breathing in and breathing out" process that allows the liquid to pass through the charred oak and its caramelized under-layer, picking up vanilla and dark sugar notes along the way, and developing that deep, rounded aspect of taste the Japanese know as umami. The maturation of the barrels is watched closely, and when ready to be bottled, our master distiller knows exactly which barrels to use to produce the full panoply of flavors that characterize the distinctive taste of Woodford Reserve. These barrels are mingled with original Woodford Reserve honey barrels from our Jefferson County distillery in a proprietary batch process that enables Woodford Reserve to exhibit its award winning taste on a consistent basis.

There are a number of aromas and flavors associated with a fine bourbon and you can find them all in Woodford Reserve—one reason why this bourbon is such a remarkably versatile ingredient in cooking.

The confectionary flavors are vanilla, caramel, honey and butterscotch, and they not only lend themselves artfully to desserts, but can provide the perfect harmonic note to sweet shellfish, such as scallops, or to full-bodied meats.

Fruit and floral flavors–apple, pear, figs, raisins, dates, citrus and rose–come forward in sauces, marinades and cocktails where the actual fruits and flowers would be used. Spice flavors, such as black pepper, tobacco leaf, nutmeg, clove and cinnamon are enhanced by the Woodford Reserve mash bill, which has a high rye component.

It's not unexpected that a distillate aged in white oak would develop woody notes, among them cedar and pine. And at the heart of it all are the distinctive grain flavors of corn, malt and rye, rounded out further with hints of almond and walnuts.

You needn't take our word for all of this when it's so simple and delightful to discover all of these flavors in your own bourbon tasting at home. You will need a bottle of Woodford Reserve, tulip stemmed nosing glasses if available (although a rocks glass will do) and some fresh water and salt-free crackers for refreshing your palate between sips.

Pour about one ounce of Woodford Reserve into your glass and begin by noting its color. The luminous orange-honey color is a sign of the bourbon's maturation. Too light and the bourbon will not have aged enough and may bite too much; too dark and it may have been in the barrel too long, becoming astringent. But just right, as the rich, robust amber of Woodford Reserve indicates, and it has a perfect balance.

Swirl the glass two or three times to open up the aroma of the bourbon and then take three short sniffs. It's tempting to take one deep breath of the intoxicating aroma, but the short sniffs are what you want in order to savor the multiple aromas–at least 15–in Woodford Reserve.

Then take a first small sip, allowing the bourbon to coat your tongue for a moment before swallowing. This taste is an explosion of pure distilled pleasure, hitting a number of taste buds in their sweetest spots. Give yourself some time to see how many of the different flavors you can recognize in just one sip. Follow with a second, slower sip and now contemplate the finish of the bourbon, savoring its long and pleasant warmth and the deep, lingering caramel notes.

Now that you've discovered the many flavors of Woodford Reserve, refer to the Culinary Flavor Wheel, to discover how to make the most of this ingredient in the kitchen.

Liquid Bourbon Ball

1 serving

2 ounces Woodford Reserve
bourbon
1 ounce white crème de cacao
1/4 ounce hazelnut liqueur
chocolate shavings

Pour the bourbon and liqueurs over
ice in a mixing glass and stir. Strain
into a chilled cocktail glass and
garnish with chocolate shavings.

Ultimate Southern Sweet Iced Tea

Chef Patrick Colley, Louisville Country Club, Louisville, Kentucky

1 serving

4 1/2 ounces unsweetened iced tea
2 1/4 ounces Ginger Syrup (page 73)
1 1/2 ounces Woodford Reserve bourbon
1 1/2 ounces peach schnapps
juice of 1 small lime wedge
1 fresh peach wedge

Combine the iced tea, syrup, bourbon, schnapps and lime juice in a cocktail shaker and shake to mix. Fill one 14-ounce tumbler **3/4** full with ice. Pour the iced tea mixture over the ice and garnish with the peach wedge.

Zinger

*Chef Brian C. Jennings, Hyatt
Regency, Lexington, Kentucky*

*A decidedly upbeat dinner
cocktail featuring Woodford
Reserve bourbon, Hibiscus
Tisane, angostura bitters, an
orange twist, and a lemon grass
swizzle stick.*

1 serving

Hibiscus Tisane
4 ounces water
2 ounces sugar
1 ounce fresh lemon juice
1 ounce fresh lime juice
1 tablespoon dried hibiscus
   flowers
1 stalk lemon grass, coarsely
   chopped

Cocktail
2 ounces Woodford Reserve
   bourbon
3 dashes bitters
1 orange twist
1 (6-inch) stalk lemon grass
   (optional)
1 hibiscus flower (optional)

For the tisane, combine the water,
sugar, lemon juice, lime juice,
hibiscus flowers and lemon grass in
a small saucepan and mix well.
Cook over medium heat for
1 minute or until the sugar dissolves,
stirring occasionally. Remove from
the heat and cool for 15 to 20
minutes; strain. You may store in
the refrigerator for up to 1 week.

   For the cocktail, pour 3 ounces of
the tisane, the bourbon and bitters
over ice in a highball glass. Tie the
orange twist around the lemon grass
stalk, add to the cocktail and stir.
Garnish with 1 hibiscus flower.

Hot Bourbon Cider

1 serving

4 ounces apple cider
11/2 ounces Woodford Reserve
   bourbon
1/2 ounce Ginger Syrup (page 73)
1/4 ounce amaretto
1/4 ounce white crème de cacao
1/16 teaspoon ground cinnamon
1 cinnamon stick

Heat the apple cider in a saucepan
until hot. Combine the bourbon,
syrup, liqueurs and ground
cinnamon in an Irish coffee mug and
mix well. Add the hot cider to the
bourbon mixture and stir. Garnish
with the cinnamon stick.

Jicama's Manhattan

Executive Chef/Owner Anthony Lamas, Jicama Grill, Louisville, Kentucky

Winner, Grand Prize

1 serving

2 ounces Woodford Reserve
   bourbon
1 ounce sweet vermouth
2 dashes of bitters
   splash of cherry juice
1 pineapple and cherry skewer

Pour the bourbon, vermouth and bitters over ice in a mixing glass and stir. Strain into a chilled cocktail glass and add a splash of cherry juice. Garnish with the fruit skewer.

Melon Splash

1 serving

1 1/2 ounces Woodford Reserve
   bourbon
1 ounce lemon-lime soda
1/2 ounce Midori
1 lime slice

Mix the bourbon, soda and liqueur
in a mixing glass and pour over ice
in a glass. Garnish with the lime slice

Mint Julep

1 serving

1 cup sugar
1 cup water
12 sprigs of mint
3 ounces Woodford Reserve
  bourbon
1 sprig of mint

Bring the sugar and water to a boil in a saucepan and boil for 5 minutes; do not stir. Pour over the 12 sprigs of mint in a heatproof bowl, gently crushing the mint with the back of a spoon. Chill, covered, for 8 to 10 hours. Strain, discarding the mint. You may store the syrup in the refrigerator for several weeks, preparing individual juleps as desired.

For each serving, fill a silver, copper, pewter or stoneware julep cup with broken or crushed ice. Add 2 tablespoons of the mint syrup and the bourbon and stir gently until the cup is frosted. Garnish with 1 sprig of mint.

New Old-Fashioned

1 serving

1 tablespoon simple syrup
5 dashes of bitters
1 peach slice
21/2 ounces Woodford Reserve
   bourbon
ice cubes
1 peach slice
2 blackberries
splash of sparkling water

Muddle the simple syrup, bitters and
1 peach slice in the bottom of an
old-fashioned glass. Add the
bourbon, ice cubes, 1 peach slice,
the blackberries and sparkling water
and stir to combine.

Bourbon Slush

20 servings

1 (46-ounce) can pineapple juice
2 (12-ounce) cans frozen
  lemonade concentrate
1 (12-ounce) can frozen orange
  juice concentrate
3 cups Woodford Reserve
bourbon
2 cups strong black tea
1 1/2 cups sugar
ginger ale
maraschino cherries
lemon or orange slices

Combine the pineapple juice,
lemonade concentrate, orange juice
concentrate, bourbon, tea and sugar
in a large freezer container and mix
well. Freeze for 8 to 10 hours,
stirring every 2 hours.

Prior to serving, let the frozen
mixture stand at room temperature
for several minutes to thaw. Stir or
mash with a potato masher until of a
slushy consistency. Scoop some of
the slush mixture into each glass and
top off with ginger ale. Garnish each
serving with a cherry and lemon or
orange slice.

Champagne Cocktail

1 serving

1 ounce Woodford Reserve
  bourbon
1/2 ounce Vanilla Syrup (page 73)
4 ounces Korbel Champagne
1/2 vanilla bean

Mix the bourbon and syrup in a
Champagne flute and top off with
the Champagne. Garnish with the
vanilla bean.

Ginger Tropics Martini

Culinary Director/Owner Jim Gerhardt, Limestone Restaurant, Louisville, Kentucky

1 serving

Bourbon Candied Ginger
4 ounces water
2 ounces Woodford Reserve bourbon
1/4 cup cane sugar
1 large piece fresh gingerroot, peeled and cut into 1/8-inch slices
cane sugar
Martini
11/2 ounces Woodford Reserve bourbon
1/2 ounce Ginger Syrup
1/4 ounce Triple Sec, or to taste

For the ginger, combine the water, bourbon and 1/4 cup cane sugar in a heavy saucepan and cook over medium heat until the sugar dissolves, stirring occasionally. Add the sliced ginger and increase the heat to high. Cook until the mixture comes to a boil and reduce the heat to low. Simmer until the mixture is reduced to a thick syrup. Remove the ginger slices to a bowl of cane sugar using a slotted spoon and toss to coat. Let stand until cool.

For the martini, pour the bourbon, syrup and liqueur over ice in a mixing glass and stir. Strain into a chilled cocktail glass and garnish with 1 slice of the Bourbon Candied Ginger.

Portofino

Chef Nat Tate, Portofino Restaurant, Lexington, Kentucky

1 serving

21/2 ounces Woodford Reserve bourbon
1 ounce peach schnapps
1/2 ounce orange juice
dash lime juice

Combine the bourbon, schnapps, orange juice and lime juice with ice in a cocktail shaker and shake to combine. Strain into a chilled martini glass.

Kentucky Peach Stand

Craig Thompson, Former Chef at Harper's Restaurant, Louisville, Kentucky

1 serving

31/4 ounces peach nectar
2 ounces Woodford Reserve bourbon
3/4 ounce Southern Comfort
1 peach slice
1 maraschino cherry

Mix the nectar, bourbon and liqueur in a cocktail shaker and shake to mix. Pour over crushed ice in a large wine glass. Thread the peach slice and cherry on a skewer and add to the cocktail.

Grand Wood 43

Chef Peng S. Looi, Asiatique and August Moon Chinese Bistro, Louisville, Kentucky

1 serving

1 ounce Woodford Reserve bourbon
1 ounce Licor 43
1 ounce Grand Marnier
ice cubes

Pour the bourbon and liqueurs over ice in a mixing glass and stir. Strain into a cocktail glass.

Ginger-Spiked Orangeade

Executive Chef John Castro, Winston's Restaurant, Louisville, Kentucky

1 serving

51/2 ounces ginger ale
11/2 ounces Woodford Reserve bourbon
1/2 ounce Triple Sec
ice cubes
1 orange twist

Combine the ginger ale, bourbon, liqueur and ice cubes in a cocktail shaker and shake to mix. Strain into one 8-ounce rocks glass and garnish with the orange twist.

Bourbon Drop

Chef Rodney Jones, Rossi's Restaurant, Lexington, Kentucky

1 serving

5 ounces Woodford Reserve bourbon
3/4 ounce simple syrup
1 teaspoon lemon juice
1 candy lemon drop
1 sprig of fresh mint

Combine the bourbon, simple syrup and lemon juice in a cocktail shaker and shake vigorously. Pour into a chilled martini glass and garnish with the lemon drop and sprig of mint.

Louisville Metro

Chef Tres Hundertmark, Clements Catering, Louisville, Kentucky

4 servings

4 ounces Woodford Reserve bourbon
1/2 ounce Ginger Syrup (page 73)
1/8 teaspoon vanilla extract (made with Woodford Reserve bourbon)
2 vanilla beans, cut into halves

Combine the bourbon, syrup and vanilla in a cocktail shaker filled with ice and shake to mix. Strain into 4 martini glasses and garnish each with 1/2 of a vanilla bean.

The Midway Front Porch Social Sip

Chef/Owner Ouita Michel, Holly Hill Inn, Midway, Kentucky

Winner, Grand Prize, and Co-Winner, "Best Written Recipe"

2 servings

1 cup water
1 any flavor tea bag
3 tablespoons sugar
4 large sprigs of mint
3 ounces Woodford Reserve bourbon
1/4 cup fresh orange juice
2 tablespoons fresh lemon juice (about 1 lemon)
1 tablespoon blond Lillet (optional)

Combine the water, tea bag, sugar and 2 sprigs of the mint in a small saucepan. Simmer over low heat until the sugar dissolves, stirring occasionally. Remove from the heat and let steep for 10 minutes. Discard the tea bag and mint and stir in the bourbon, orange juice, lemon juice and Lillet. Pour over ice in 2 large iced tea glasses and garnish with the remaining 2 sprigs of mint.

Ginger Syrup

Makes 2 cups

2 cups sugar
1 cup water
1 cup thinly sliced peeled fresh gingerroot

Bring the sugar, water and gingerroot to a boil in a saucepan and reduce the heat. Simmer for 3 minutes, stirring occasionally. Remove from the heat and let stand until cool. Strain into a covered container and store in the refrigerator for up to 1 week. The ginger flavor will fade with age.

Vanilla Syrup

Makes 1 cup

2 cups sugar
1 cup water
2 vanilla beans

Bring the sugar and water to a boil in a saucepan. Split the vanilla beans lengthwise into halves and place in a heatproof jar or bottle. Pour the hot syrup over the vanilla beans and let stand for 8 to 10 hours. Store in the refrigerator for up to 1 week.

Infused Cherries

Variable servings

1 jar maraschino cherries
Woodford Reserve bourbon

Drain the cherries and return the cherries to the jar. Fill the jar with the bourbon. Let stand, covered, for 1 to 2 weeks before serving.

APPETIZERS

Pickled Shrimp

Chef/Owner Ouita Michel, Holly Hill Inn, Midway, Kentucky

Some great southern hostesses spend a lifetime perfecting their pickled shrimp recipe. Tinker no more! Chef Ouita has created the perfect balance of seafood and seasonings here. All you need now is a tray of Woodford Old-Fashioned cocktails on the rocks for the perfect cocktail hour.

12 to 16 servings

3 pounds fresh extra-large shrimp, or 2 pounds cooked frozen shrimp
salt to taste
4 cups thinly sliced white onions
1 cup vegetable oil
1 cup fresh lemon juice
1 cup apple cider vinegar
2 tablespoons sugar
5 bay leaves
1 teaspoon crushed black peppercorns
1 teaspoon dill seeds
1 teaspoon celery salt
1 teaspoon dry mustard
1/2 teaspoon cayenne pepper
1/2 teaspoon tarragon

Peel and devein the fresh shrimp. Combine the shrimp, salt and enough water to generously cover in a large saucepan. Steam or gently simmer for 3 to 5 minutes or just until the shrimp turn pink and are cooked through. If using frozen shrimp, just thaw. Layer the shrimp and onions alternately in a nonreactive dish.

Whisk the oil, lemon juice, vinegar, sugar, bay leaves, peppercorns, dill seeds, celery salt, dry mustard, cayenne pepper and tarragon in a saucepan and bring to a simmer. Simmer for 10 minutes. Remove from the heat and cool slightly. Pour the warm marinade over the shrimp and onions and let stand until cool. Marinate, covered, in the refrigerator for 4 to 48 hours, stirring occasionally. The flavor of the shrimp is enhanced if allowed to marinate for 48 hours. Discard the bay leaves and marinade before serving.

Steak Bites

Woodford Reserve's kitchen

Hearty and savory appetizers–or you can make the filling and sauce and pile it all in split French rolls for a delicious lunch for four.

Makes 3 dozen steak bites

1 cup Woodford Reserve bourbon
2 pounds filet mignon
salt and freshly ground pepper to taste
2 tablespoons olive oil
2 tablespoons butter
1 large white onion, sliced
1 large red onion, sliced
1 baguette French bread, cut into 1/4 to 1/2 inch slices
1/2 cup crumbled blue cheese
1/2 cup sour cream
1 bunch flat-leaf parsley, trimmed
3/4 cup grape tomatoes, cut into halves or quarters

Pour the bourbon over the filet in a shallow dish, turning to coat. Marinate in the refrigerator for 1 hour, turning occasionally. Drain, discarding the marinade, and season to taste with salt and pepper.

Preheat the oven to 350 degrees. Heat the olive oil in a large ovenproof sauté pan. Add the filet to the hot oil and sear for 1 minute per side. Roast for 15 minutes or until a meat thermometer registers 145 degrees for medium-rare.

Let rest for 15 minutes. Cut the filet lengthwise into halves and cut each half into 18 thin slices for a total of 36 slices.

Heat the butter in a large sauté pan over medium-low heat. Add the onions and cook for 25 minutes or until the onions are deep golden brown in color and caramelized, stirring occasionally. Preheat the broiler. Arrange the bread slices in a single layer on a baking sheet and broil until brown on both sides. Mix the cheese and sour cream in a bowl.

To serve, arrange 1 filet slice on each toasted baguette slice. Layer each with some of the caramelized onions and a dollop of the cheese mixture. Top with a sprig of parsley and a tomato half.

Country Ham and Asparagus Tartlets

Woodford Reserve's kitchen

Spring is celebrated in Kentucky the minute the first asparagus spears appear in the garden. Use fine Kentucky country ham and serve with one of the Woodford Reserve cocktails, and you'll have the full flavor of the region in a couple of bites.

Makes 18 tartlets

Pastry
3 ounces cream cheese, softened
1/4 cup (1/2 stick) butter, softened
3/4 cup flour
1/4 cup cornmeal

Filling and Assembly
3/4 cup (3 ounces) shredded
  fontina cheese
1 tablespoon flour
1/3 cup half-and-half
1 egg
1/2 cup finely chopped
  country ham
2 tablespoons finely chopped red
  bell pepper
18 fresh asparagus tips, 3/4 inch
  long

For the pastry, using a fork or pastry blender, mix the cream cheese and butter in a bowl until blended. Stir in the flour and cornmeal and chill, covered, for 1 hour. Shape the pastry into eighteen 1-inch balls. Press each ball over the bottom and up the side of a miniature muffin cup and chill for 30 minutes.

For the filling, preheat the oven to 425 degrees. Combine the cheese and flour in a bowl and mix well. Whisk the half-and-half and egg in a bowl until blended. Stir the cheese mixture, ham and bell pepper into the egg mixture and spoon evenly into the pastry-lined muffin cups. Bake for 7 minutes and reduce the oven temperature to 325 degrees. Top each tartlet with an asparagus tip and bake for 5 minutes longer or until set.

Chicken Quesadillas

Chef Mark Williams,
Brown-Forman Corporation,
Louisville, Kentucky

Makes 32 appetizer quesadillas

2 tablespoons vegetable oil
11/2 cups thinly sliced red onions
1 teaspoon minced jalapeño chile
2 tablespoons minced garlic
4 cups shredded cooked rotisserie
   chicken (3-pounds chicken)
1/3 cup fresh cilantro, chopped
1 tablespoon cumin
1/4 cup Woodford Reserve
   bourbon
salt and pepper to taste
8 (7-inch) flour tortillas
4 ounces Monterey Jack cheese,
   shredded
4 ounces sharp Cheddar cheese,
   shredded
6 tablespoons vegetable oil

Heat 2 tablespoons oil in a medium sauté pan over medium heat. Add the onions and jalapeño chile to the hot oil and cook for 5 minutes or until tender, stirring frequently. Stir in the garlic and cook for 1 minute, stirring frequently. Add the chicken, cilantro and cumin and cook just until the chicken is heated through, stirring occasionally. Stir in the bourbon and increase the heat to high. Cook until the liquid is reduced to 1 tablespoon, stirring occasionally. Season to taste with salt and pepper.

Spread 3/4 cup of the chicken mixture over 1/2 of each tortilla.

Sprinkle each with 2 tablespoons of the Monterey Jack cheese and 2 tablespoons of the Cheddar cheese and fold over to enclose the filling.

Heat 6 tablespoons oil in a sauté pan over high heat until smoking. Reduce the heat to medium and brown the quesadillas in batches in the hot oil for 4 minutes or until the cheese melts and the quesadillas are brown, turning once. Remove the quesadillas to a cutting board and cut each into fourths. Serve with salsa, guacamole and sour cream.

Chicken Liver Pâté

Woodford Reserve's kitchen

The full notes of a fine bourbon followed by just a hint of bite from the rye are the perfect undercurrents for this rich pâté. We warrant you'll be impressed.

8 to 10 servings

1/2 cup (1 stick) unsalted butter
1 cup finely chopped onion
1 large garlic clove, minced
1 pound chicken livers, trimmed
   and cut into halves
1 teaspoon minced fresh thyme
1 teaspoon minced fresh sage
3/4 teaspoon salt
1/4 teaspoon pepper
1/8 teaspoon allspice
2 tablespoons Woodford Reserve
   bourbon

Heat the butter in a large nonstick skillet over medium-low heat. Add the onion and garlic to the butter and cook for 5 minutes or until the onion is tender, stirring frequently. Stir in the livers, thyme, sage, salt, pepper and allspice and cook for 2 minutes per side or until the livers are still pink internally. Remove from the heat.

Immediately pour the bourbon over the liver mixture and carefully ignite. Return the skillet to the heat and swirl until the flames subside. Process the liver mixture in a food processor until smooth. Spoon pâté into a crock and smooth the top. Press plastic wrap directly on the surface and chill for 2 hours or until firm. Serve chilled or at room temperature with party bread or assorted party crackers.

Corn and Crab Fritters

Chef Mark Williams, Brown-Forman Corporation, Louisville, Kentucky

Makes 2 dozen fritters

Tartar Sauce
1/2 cup mayonnaise
2 tablespoons chopped dill pickles
1 tablespoon fresh lemon juice
1 tablespoon chopped fresh
   parsley
1 teaspoon Dijon mustard

Fritters
6 tablespoons cornmeal
1/2 cup plus 2 tablespoons flour
1 teaspoon baking powder
1/2 teaspoon salt
1/2 cup milk
2 tablespoons vegetable oil
1 egg, beaten
1/4 cup chopped scallions
1/4 cup finely chopped red bell
   pepper
1 tablespoon minced garlic
2 tablespoons vegetable oil
1 cup blue crab claw meat, shells
   removed
1/2 cup fresh corn kernels
1/3 cup Woodford Reserve
   bourbon
1 teaspoon cayenne pepper
vegetable oil for frying

For the sauce, combine the mayonnaise, pickles, lemon juice, parsley and Dijon mustard in a bowl and mix well. Store, covered, in the refrigerator.

For the fritters, mix the cornmeal, flour, baking powder and salt in a bowl. Add the milk, 2 tablespoons oil, the egg and scallions. Stir just until moistened. Sauté the bell pepper and garlic in 2 tablespoons oil in a medium sauté pan until the bell pepper is tender. Stir in the crab meat, corn and bourbon. Increase the heat and cook until the liquid is reduced by 1/2, stirring frequently. Remove from the heat and stir in the cayenne pepper. Let stand until cool and stir into the cornmeal mixture.

Pour enough oil into a large skillet or saucepan to measure 1/2 inch and heat to 350 degrees. Using a tablespoon or small scoop, drop enough batter for 5 to 6 fritters into the hot oil. Fry for 2 minutes per side or until golden brown. Remove the fritters to paper towels to drain. Repeat the process with the remaining batter. Serve warm with the Tartar Sauce. You may prepare the fritters in advance and store, covered, in the refrigerator. Reheat at 350 degrees for 8 minutes

Kentucky Pizza

David Larson, Chef-in-Residence, Woodford Reserve Distillery, Versailles, Kentucky

Who needs imported ham when you have the pride of Kentucky's smokehouses to give this Italian classic a regional spin?

Makes 1 (9-inch) pizza

Pizza Crust
1 teaspoon dry yeast
1/2 cup plus 1 tablespoon war
   (105- to 110-degree) water
13/8 cups flour
1/4 cup cornmeal
2 teaspoons sugar
1 teaspoon salt
1 tablespoon plus 1 teaspoon
   extra-virgin olive oil

Topping and Assembly
cornmeal
1 cup thinly sliced mushrooms
3 tablespoons sliced scallions
1 garlic clove, minced
2 tablespoons olive oil
1/2 cup (2 ounces) shredded
   mozzarella cheese
1/4 cup finely chopped country ham
2 ounces goat cheese, crumbled
1 teaspoon finely chopped fresh
   sage
1 teaspoon finely chopped fresh
   rosemary
cracked ground black pepper to
   taste
2 cups baby arugula, mâche or
   other fresh seasonal salad
   greens
2 teaspoons olive oil

For the crust, dissolve the yeast in the warm water; let stand for 5 to 10 minutes. Mix in a mixing bowl the flour, cornmeal, sugar, salt and 1 tablespoon of the olive oil and stir in the yeast mixture. Beat with an electric mixer fitted with a paddle attachment at low speed for 2 minutes or until the dough is smooth and elastic. The dough should be slightly tacky. Beat in an additional 1 to 2 tablespoons flour if the dough is too sticky; do not overmix. If mixing by hand, combine the dry ingredients in a large bowl and make a well in the center of the ingredients. Pour the yeast mixture and 1 tablespoon of the oil into the well and stir with a wooden spoon until combined, adding an additional 1 to 2 tablespoons flour if the dough is too sticky. Knead on a lightly floured surface for 5 minutes; the dough should be slightly tacky. Shape the dough into a ball.

Coat a 1-quart bowl with the remaining 1 teaspoon olive oil. Place the dough ball in the oiled bowl, turning to coat. Let stand, covered with plastic wrap, at room temperature for 11/2 to 2 hours or until doubled in bulk. Punch down the dough and reshape into a ball in the same bowl. Chill, covered with plastic wrap, for 8 to 10 hours.

Remove the dough from the refrigerator 2 hours before assembling the pizza. Divide the dough into 2 equal portions. Roll each portion into a ball on a smooth clean surface, sealing any holes by pinching or rolling. Arrange the dough balls in a glass dish. Allow enough room between the dough balls for each to double in bulk. Let stand, covered with plastic wrap, at room temperature for 2 hours.

For the topping, preheat a pizza stone on the center oven rack at 500 degrees for 1 hour. Maintain the oven temperature. Roll the dough into a 9-inch round on a lightly floured board or cloth. Lightly sprinkle cornmeal over the surface of a wooden pizza peel and arrange the dough round over the cornmeal.

Sauté the mushrooms, scallions and garlic in 1 tablespoon of the olive oil in a sauté pan until tender. Immediately brush the pizza round with the remaining 1 tablespoon olive oil and sprinkle with the mozzarella cheese, mushroom mixture, ham, goat cheese, sage, rosemary and pepper. Work quickly to place the toppings on the crust so the pizza does not become soggy. Jerk the crust slightly to assure that it will come off the peel easily. Position the edge of the peel over the center of the heated pizza stone and jiggle the peel to slide the crust off and then quickly pull the peel out from under the pizza. Bake for 8 to 10 minutes or until the crust is crisp and golden brown. Remove the pizza from the oven and top with the arugula. Drizzle with 2 teaspoons olive oil and grind cracked pepper over the top. Cut into wedges and serve immediately. You may substitute your favorite thin crust recipe for the crust recipe above.

New Fangled Tomato Dumplings

Chef/Owner Ouita Michel, Holly Hill Inn, Midway, Kentucky

Remember the comfort of buttered tomatoes baked in a casserole with soft bread? You'll find the same satisfaction here, but embellished elegantly with the use of goat cheese or ricotta and a pastry crust. These make a hearty opener for the meal to follow, or can also serve as a side dish.

4 servings as a first course or light entrée

2 large or 4 small tomatoes
salt and freshly ground pepper to taste
4 ounces goat cheese, feta cheese or ricotta cheese, softened
2 tablespoons freshly minced dill weed, basil or parsley
2 green onions, minced
2 sheets frozen puff pastry, thawed
1 egg
2 tablespoons water
1/4 cup cider vinegar
1/4 cup packed brown sugar

Preheat the oven to 375 degrees. Cut around the stem of each tomato and remove. Cut a small "x" in the opposite end of each tomato. Bring a saucepan of water to a boil and fill a bowl with ice water. Plunge the tomatoes into the boiling water and let stand for 10 seconds or until their skins loosen. Immediately remove from the boiling water and plunge into the ice water.

Drain and peel the tomatoes. If working with large tomatoes, cut into halves, remove the seeds and core gently without leaving too big of a hole. If using smaller tomatoes, cut off the top fourth of the tomato and gently spoon out the seeds. Pat the tomatoes dry with paper towels and sprinkle the inside of the tomatoes with salt and pepper. Invert onto paper towels and drain for 30 minutes.

Combine the goat cheese, dill weed and green onions in a bowl and mix well. Season to taste with salt and pepper. Spoon 2 to 3 tablespoons of the cheese mixture into each tomato. Cut the pastry sheets into 4 squares large enough to enclose the tomatoes, allowing 2 inches on each side.

Place 1 tomato half or tomato in the center of each pastry square and cut slits in the pastry from each corner towards the center. Whisk the egg and water in a bowl until blended and brush the pastry with the egg wash. Bring the triangles up around the tomatoes, pressing them together at the top and using scraps of pastry to cover all the edges. It is acceptable to allow a small portion of the tomato to peek through. Brush the outside of the dumplings with the remaining egg wash. Arrange the dumplings on a baking sheet. Mix the vinegar and brown sugar in a small saucepan. Simmer for 5 minutes, stirring occasionally.

Remove from the heat.

Bake the dumplings for 15 minutes or until golden brown and crispy, basting with the vinegar syrup occasionally, or drizzle the warm vinegar syrup over the dumplings after baking. You may substitute cherry tomatoes for the larger tomatoes for a great party appetizer.

Scampi Crostini

Chef Rodney Jones, Rossi's Restaurant, Lexington, Kentucky

The complex flavor created by the bourbon in the scampi sauce belies the simplicity of making this delightful appetizer. Serve it at the start of a cozy supper for friends.

4 servings

6 slices white bread, crusts
 trimmed
4 teaspoons butter
24 large prawns, peeled and
 deveined
4 teaspoons chopped shallots
4 teaspoons tomato paste
kosher salt and freshly ground
pepper to taste
2 cups Woodford Reserve
 bourbon
2 cups heavy cream
chopped fresh parsley
lemon wedges

Preheat the broiler. Cut each bread slice into 4 triangles and arrange on a baking sheet. Broil until brown on both sides.

Heat the butter in an 8-inch sauté pan. Sauté the prawns in the butter over medium-high heat for 30 seconds. Add the shallots and sauté for 30 seconds. Stir in the tomato paste, salt and pepper and sauté for 1 minute longer. Remove the prawns to a heated platter using a slotted spoon, reserving the pan juices.

Deglaze the sauté pan with the bourbon. Return the prawns to the

sauté pan and stir in the heavy cream. Cook for 2 minutes, stirring frequently. Remove the prawns with a slotted spoon and arrange 1 prawn on each toast point, reserving the cream mixture.

Cook the reserved cream mixture until it coats the back of a spoon, stirring frequently. Drizzle the sauce over the prawns and garnish each with parsley and a lemon wedge.

"You cannot do better than Woodford Reserve. It's no ordinary bourbon. It's like a wine. You don't use an inferior wine when you cook. And I love to cook with bourbon, so I'm going to use the one that brings the most complexity to the recipe."

Chef Anthony Lamas

SIDES &
SALADS

Woodford Wilt

David Larson, Chef-in-Residence, Woodford Reserve Distillery, Versailles, Kentucky

Wilted lettuce is a simple dish from the country that was used as a side salad, or served as the main dish in summertime with a pan of corn bread on the side. To do the latter, you can make this elegant version even heartier with the addition of grilled chicken strips.

4 servings

1 cup fresh corn kernels (about 2 ears) or frozen white Shoe Peg corn kernels
2 tablespoons cornstarch
2 tablespoons flour
1 cup drained hominy
2 tablespoons vegetable oil
3 slices bacon
1 tablespoon chopped shallots
1 teaspoon sugar
1 tablespoon Woodford Reserve bourbon
1 tablespoon vegetable oil
1 tablespoon cider vinegar
2 teaspoons sugar
6 cups mixed seasonal salad greens, such as watercress, escarole, arugula
2 tablespoons chopped red bell pepper
2 tablespoons sliced kalamata olives (optional)
salt and freshly ground pepper to taste

Blanch the corn in boiling water in a saucepan for 1 minute; drain. Mix the cornstarch and flour in a bowl and stir in the hominy.

Place the hominy mixture in a sieve and shake to remove the excess flour mixture. Sauté the hominy in 2 tablespoons oil in a medium sauté pan over medium heat for 3 to 4 minutes or until a crust forms; do not want a mushy consistency.

Fry the bacon in a skillet until brown and crisp. Remove the bacon to a bowl and coarsely crumble, reserving the bacon drippings. Cool the drippings for several minutes and stir in the shallots and 1 teaspoon sugar. Cook over low heat until caramelized, stirring frequently. Increase the heat to high and stir in the bourbon. Cook for 30 seconds. Reduce the heat and stir in 1 tablespoon oil, the vinegar and 2 teaspoons sugar. Cook until heated through, stirring occasionally.

Toss the corn, hominy, bacon, salad greens, bell pepper and olives in a bowl and drizzle with the warm dressing. Season to taste with salt and pepper and serve immediately. Add chopped grilled chicken for a nice entrée salad.

Sweet-and-Sour Asparagus Salad

David Larson, Chef-in-Residence, Woodford Reserve Distillery, Versailles, Kentucky

8 to 10 servings

Sweet-and-Sour Dressing
2/3 cup distilled vinegar
1/2 cup sugar
3 cinnamon sticks
1 tablespoon celery seeds
1 teaspoon whole cloves
1/2 teaspoon salt

Salad
48 fresh asparagus spears, trimmed
1 red bell pepper, julienned
1/2 small red onion, thinly sliced and separated into rings
1 romaine heart, coarsely torn

For the dressing, bring the vinegar, sugar, cinnamon sticks, celery seeds, cloves and salt to a boil in a saucepan and boil until the sugar dissolves, stirring occasionally. Strain into a heatproof bowl, discarding the solids.

For the salad, steam the asparagus in a steamer for 2 to 5 minutes or until tender-crisp. Immediately plunge the asparagus into an ice bath to stop the cooking process. Drain and pat dry with paper towels.

Arrange the asparagus, bell pepper and onion in a shallow dish. Pour the warm dressing over the asparagus mixture and turn to coat. Let stand for 25 minutes and drain. Line a platter with the romaine and top with the asparagus mixture.

Glenn's Creek Summer Cucumber Salad

David Larson, Chef-in-Residence, Woodford Reserve Distillery, Versailles, Kentucky

10 servings

8 ounces bacon, crisp-cooked and crumbled
2 cups sour cream
2 tablespoons cider vinegar
1/4 cup chopped fresh chives
1 tablespoon sugar
2 garlic cloves, finely chopped
2 teaspoons Woodford Reserve bourbon
1 teaspoon salt
1/2 teaspoon freshly ground pepper
6 cucumbers, peeled and thinly sliced

Combine the bacon, sour cream, vinegar, chives, sugar, garlic, bourbon, salt and pepper in a bowl and mix well. Add the cucumbers and mix gently. Serve immediately.

Corn Relish

*Chef Mark Williams,
Brown-Forman Corporation,
Louisville, Kentucky*

16 servings

12 ears of corn
2 cups chopped red bell peppers
2 cups chopped green bell
    peppers
2 cups chopped celery
1 cup chopped onion
31/4 cups vinegar
11/3 cups sugar
2 tablespoons pickling or
    canning salt
2 teaspoons celery seeds
2 tablespoons dry mustard
1 teaspoon turmeric
1/3 cup Woodford Reserve bourbon

Boil the corn in a generous amount
of water in a stockpot for 5 minutes.
Drain and plunge into a large bowl
of cold water to stop the cooking
process; drain. Cut the tops of the
corn kernels with a sharp knife into
a bowl.

Bring the bell peppers, celery,
onion, vinegar, sugar, salt and celery
seeds to a boil in a saucepan,
stirring occasionally. Reduce the heat
to low and simmer for 5 minutes,
stirring occasionally. Mix the dry
mustard and turmeric in a bowl. Stir
1/2 cup of the bell pepper mixture
into the dry mustard mixture. Stir the
dry mustard mixture, bourbon and
corn into the hot bell pepper
mixture and mix well. Simmer for
5 minutes, stirring occasionally.
Serve at room temperature or chilled.

Savory Corn Cake

*Linda Nee, Woodford Reserve's
kitchen*

10 to 12 servings

1 cup sugar
1 cup yellow cornmeal
1 cup flour
4 teaspoons baking powder
1/2 teaspoon salt
1 (17-ounce) can cream-style corn
1 cup (2 sticks) unsalted butter,
    softened
4 eggs, lightly beaten
1/2 cup (2 ounces) shredded
    Monterey Jack cheese
1/2 cup (2 ounces) shredded
    Cheddar cheese

Preheat the oven to 400 degrees.
Coat a 9×13-inch baking pan with
butter or spray with nonstick
cooking spray. Combine the sugar,
cornmeal, flour, baking powder and
salt in a bowl and mix well. Add the
corn, 1 cup butter, eggs, Monterey
Jack cheese and Cheddar cheese and
mix well. Spoon the cornmeal
mixture into the prepared pan.

Bake for 35 minutes or until a
wooden pick inserted in the center
comes out clean and the top is
golden brown. Cool in the pan on a
wire rack before slicing.

Asparagus with Kentucky Hollandaise Sauce

David Larson, Chef-in-Residence, Woodford Reserve Distillery, Versailles, Kentucky

6 servings

2 pounds fresh asparagus, trimmed
1/2 cup (1 stick) unsalted butter
3 egg yolks
2 tablespoons fresh lemon juice
1 tablespoon Woodford Reserve bourbon
salt and pepper to taste
3 tablespoons chopped fresh tomato

Bring a large saucepan of water to a boil, add the asparagus and return to a gentle boil. Boil for 1 to 2 minutes for tiny spears, 3 to 5 minutes for small spears, 5 to 8 minutes for medium spears and 10 to 12 minutes for large spears or until tender-crisp and bright green in color. Drain and arrange the spears on a clean tea towel to drain. If serving at room temperature, plunge the spears into an ice bath and drain.

Heat the butter in a small saucepan until melted. Remove from the heat and cool to room temperature. Fill the bottom of a double boiler with water and bring almost to a boil over high heat. Reduce the heat to low so the water is hot but not boiling. Combine the egg yolks, lemon juice and bourbon in the top of the double boiler.

Wisk until blended and place over the hot water. Cook until smooth, whisking constantly. Add the melted butter gradually, whisking constantly. If the sauce separates or curdles at this point, add 1 ice cube and whisk briskly until it melts. This will bring the sauce back together. Season to taste with salt and pepper and fold in the tomato. Drizzle the sauce over the asparagus on a serving platter and serve immediately.

Tian of Summer Vegetables

Chef/Owner Ouita Michel, Holly Hill Inn, Midway, Kentucky

A stacked deck of savory vegetables brings a medley of colors, textures, and tastes to the table. This is a divine side dish for heartier entrées, or you can serve as a vegetarian meal on its own.

4 to 6 servings

2 baking potatoes, peeled and thinly sliced
3 large tomatoes, peeled and thinly sliced
1 large eggplant, peeled and thinly sliced
2 zucchini, thinly sliced
salt and pepper to taste
1/4 cup (1/2 stick) butter, cubed
1 cup (4 ounces) grated Parmesan cheese or asiago cheese
1/2 cup white wine or chicken broth
1/2 cup panko or other bread crumbs
2 tablespoons extra-virgin olive oil
2 tablespoons minced garlic
2 tablespoons chopped fresh parsley
1 tablespoon chopped fresh thyme, or 1 teaspoon dried thyme

Preheat the oven to 375 degrees. Grease a 9×13-inch baking dish with butter or oil or spray with nonstick cooking spray. Layer the potatoes, tomatoes, eggplant and zucchini in the order listed in the prepared dish, seasoning each layer with salt and pepper, dotting with 1 tablespoon of

the butter and sprinkling with 1/4 cup of the cheese. Pour the wine down 1 side of the baking dish.

Toss the bread crumbs with the olive oil, garlic, parsley and thyme in a bowl and sprinkle the bread crumb mixture over the prepared layers. Bake for 1 hour or until the vegetables are tender and the bread crumb topping is golden brown. Let rest for 15 minutes before slicing, or let stand for 1 hour and serve. You may substitute extra-virgin olive oil for the butter. Bake in a round ceramic baker or quiche pan if desired, but the baking time must be adjusted to the size of the dish and thickness of the vegetables.

Sweet Potato Biscuits

Linda Nee, Woodford Reserve's kitchen

Makes 1 dozen (2 1/2-inch) biscuits

1 1/2 cups flour
2 tablespoons sugar
4 teaspoons baking powder
1/2 teaspoon salt
1/8 teaspoon baking soda
3/4 cup milk
3/4 cup mashed cooked sweet
  potatoes
1/4 cup shortening
2 tablespoons Woodford Reserve
  bourbon
1 tablespoon butter, melted

Preheat the oven to 425 degrees. Mix the flour, sugar, baking powder, salt and baking soda in a bowl. Combine the milk, sweet potatoes, shortening and bourbon in a bowl and mix well. Add the flour mixture to the sweet potato mixture and mix just until combined; do not overmix.

Knead the dough on a lightly floured surface for 30 seconds. Roll the dough 3/4 inch thick and cut into rounds using a 2 1/2-inch cutter. Arrange the rounds 1 inch apart on a baking sheet and bake for 12 to 15 minutes or until puffed and golden brown. Brush the tops with the butter and remove to a wire rack.

Corn Pudding Versailles

David Larson, Chef-in-Residence, Woodford Reserve Distillery, Versailles, Kentucky

So simple to prepare, but simply divine. This dish is like the elegant black dress–perfect in any context.

8 to 10 servings

4 cups fresh white corn kernels
  (about 8 ears)
1/2 cup sugar
2 teaspoons flour
1 teaspoon salt
1/2 teaspoon baking powder
6 eggs, beaten
2 cups heavy cream
1 cup half-and-half
2 tablespoons butter, melted

Preheat the oven to 350 degrees. Process 1 cup of the corn in a food processor until ground. Combine the ground corn, remaining 3 cups corn kernels, sugar, flour, salt and baking powder in a bowl and mix well. Whisk the eggs, heavy cream and half-and-half in a bowl until blended and stir into the corn mixture. Add the butter and mix well.

Pour the corn mixture into a greased 9×13-inch baking pan and bake for 40 minutes or until a sharp knife inserted in the center comes out clean. You may substitute frozen Shoe Peg corn for the fresh corn kernels.

Sweet Corn and Bacon Risotto

Chef Patrick Colley, Louisville Country Club, Louisville, Kentucky

An uptown version of the down-home classic, fresh creamed corn cooked in bacon drippings, this is an ultimate side dish or a fine main course as well.

8 side dish servings, or 4 first course servings

4 cups chicken broth
1 tablespoon vegetable oil
3 slices smoked bacon, chopped
1/2 onion, finely chopped
2 cups arborio rice
1/2 cup dry white wine
corn kernels from 3 large ears of
  corn
2 tablespoons butter
1/4 cup heavy cream
3 large green onions, finely sliced
salt and pepper to taste

Bring the broth to a simmer in a saucepan. Heat the oil in a large heavy saucepan over medium-high heat. Cook the bacon in the hot oil until the fat is rendered and the bacon is crisp. Stir in the onion and cook for 5 minutes or until the onion is tender, stirring frequently. Add the rice and cook for 1 to 2 minutes or until the rice is coated, stirring constantly. Stir in the wine and cook until the wine is absorbed, stirring frequently. Reduce the heat to medium. Reserve 1/4 cup of the hot broth.

Add 1 cup of the remaining hot broth to the rice mixture and cook until most of the broth is absorbed, stirring frequently. Add the remaining hot broth 1/2 cup at a time and cook until the broth is almost absorbed after each addition, stirring frequently. This should take about 18 minutes. Stir in the reserved broth, corn, butter and heavy cream.

Cook until the liquid is absorbed and the mixture is creamy, stirring frequently. Remove from the heat and stir in the green onions. Season to taste with salt and pepper and serve immediately. You may substitute frozen corn for the fresh corn.

Fried Green Tomatoes with Tomato Relish

David Larson, Chef-in-Residence, Woodford Reserve Distillery, Versailles, Kentucky

Plain country fare at a noontime dinner, these tomatoes dress up nicely for a party with the addition of the snappy relish.

4 servings

Tomato Relish
2 cups coarsely chopped seeded mixed red or heirloom tomatoes
2 tablespoons chopped scallions
1 tablespoon chopped fresh cilantro
1/2 small jalapeño chile, minced
1/4 cup olive oil
2 teaspoons fresh lime juice
1 garlic clove, minced
1/2 teaspoon sugar, or to taste
1/4 teaspoon cumin
salt and pepper to taste

Fried Green Tomatoes
1 cup flour
11/2 teaspoons salt
3/4 teaspoon white pepper
1 cup yellow cornmeal
1/2 teaspoon paprika
2 green tomatoes, cut into 1/2-inch slices
2 eggs, beaten
peanut oil for frying

For the relish, toss the tomatoes, scallions, cilantro and jalapeño chile in a bowl. Add the olive oil, lime juice, garlic, sugar, cumin, salt and pepper and mix until coated. Store, covered, in the refrigerator for up to 1 day. Substitute grape tomatoes in the off-season.

For the green tomatoes, mix the flour, 1 teaspoon of the salt and 1/4 teaspoon of the white pepper in a shallow dish. Mix the remaining 1/2 teaspoon salt, remaining 1/2 teaspoon pepper, cornmeal and paprika in a shallow dish. Coat the tomatoes with the flour mixture, dip in the eggs and coat with the cornmeal mixture.

Preheat the oven to 350 degrees. Heat enough peanut oil in a sauté pan to measure 1 inch. Fry the tomatoes in the hot oil until crisp and golden brown and drain on a rack. You may prepare to this point and store, covered, in the refrigerator until just before serving.

Arrange the tomato slices in a single layer on a baking sheet and bake for 8 to 10 minutes or until heated through. The tomatoes should be tender but not mushy. Remove the tomatoes to a serving platter and top with the relish. Serve immediately.

ENTRÉES

Rib-Eyes with Bacon Potato Salad and Heirloom Tomatoes

Chef Nathan Carlson,
Avalon Restaurant,
Louisville, Kentucky

A terrific piece of meat and a classic concept: If you're going to mess with that, you had better do it well. Chef Nathan Carslon raises the gold standard with this recipe.

2 servings

Bacon Potato Salad
8 ounces red potatoes, cut into quarters
2 quarts water
salt to taste
3 slices applewood smoked bacon, crisp-cooked and coarsely chopped
1/2 cup crème fraîche*
1/4 cup chopped onion
2 tablespoons minced sweet pickle
2 tablespoons spicy brown mustard
pepper to taste

Spiced Butter
1/4 cup (1/2 stick) unsalted butter, softened
1 teaspoon chipotle powder
2 teaspoons paprika
1 teaspoon dry mustard
1 teaspoon coriander
1 teaspoon ground celery seeds
salt and pepper to taste

Heirloom Tomatoes
2 heirloom tomatoes, cut into quarters
2 teaspoons minced fresh Italian parsley
2 teaspoons minced fresh chives
2 tablespoons olive oil
2 teaspoons sherry vinegar
kosher salt and freshly ground pepper to taste

The Steaks
1 cup Woodford Reserve bourbon
2 garlic cloves, minced
2 teaspoons minced fresh sage
2 (12-ounce) boneless rib-eye Delmonico steaks
1 to 2 tablespoons olive oil
kosher salt and freshly ground pepper to taste

For the potato salad, bring the potatoes, water and salt to a boil in a large saucepan. Reduce the heat and simmer until tender. Drain and place the potatoes in an ice water bath to stop the cooking process; drain.

Combine the bacon, crème fraîche, onion, pickle and mustard in a medium bowl. Add the potatoes and mix well. Season to taste with salt and pepper and store, covered, in the refrigerator until serving time. Adjust the seasonings before serving.

For the butter, combine the butter with the chipotle powder, paprika, dry mustard, coriander and celery seeds in a mixing bowl and mix well with an electric mixer or fork. Season to taste with salt and pepper.

For the tomatoes, combine the tomatoes, parsley, chives, olive oil and vinegar in a bowl and toss lightly. Season to taste with salt and pepper and let stand at room temperature.

For the steaks, combine the bourbon, garlic and sage in a bowl. Add the steaks, coating well. Marinate at room temperature for 1 hour, turning once; drain and season to taste with salt and pepper.

Heat a cast-iron skillet over medium-high heat and add the olive oil. Add the steaks and sear for 4 minutes. Turn the steaks and sear for 2 minutes longer for medium-rare.

To serve, place the steaks to 1 side of the serving plates. Add a scoop of the potato salad and arrange the tomatoes to the side. Place a dollop of the spiced butter on each steak.

*You may use commercial **Crème Fraîche** in the recipe or prepare by combining 1 cup heavy cream with 2 tablespoons buttermilk in a glass container. Let stand, covered, at 70 degrees for 8 to 24 hours or until thickened. Stir well and store, covered, in the refrigerator for up to 10 days.

"When the folks show up who have an appreciation for fine wines—well, that's when you bring out the bottle of Woodford Reserve for savoring."

Chef Brian Jennings

Grilled Lamb with Minted Couscous

Executive Chef John Castro, Winston's Restaurant, Louisville, Kentucky

This recipe delivers mouthfuls of spicy richness at the table.

6 servings

The Lamb
1/4 cup ground black peppercorns**
1 tablespoon kosher salt**
1 1/2 tablespoons coriander**
1 tablespoon cinnamon**
1 tablespoon ground cloves**
1 teaspoon cardamom
1/8 teaspoon freshly ground
  nutmeg
1/4 cup sweet paprika
24 (3/4-inch-thick) Kentucky lamb
  chops or chops cut from a
  Frenched rack of lamb

Gastrique
1/4 cup Woodford Reserve
  bourbon
1/2 cup fresh blackberry purée or
  blackberry preserves
1/4 cup Kentucky sorghum
1 bay leaf
1/2 teaspoon Korean chile flakes or
  ground seedless red chiles
1 teaspoon sugar
1/2 teaspoon salt

Sweet-and-Sour Syrup
1/4 cup Woodford Reserve
  bourbon
1/4 cup red chili sauce*
1 cup water
3/4 cup sugar
6 garlic cloves, chopped
1 tablespoon sesame oil
1 tablespoon fish sauce
1 tablespoon tamari sauce
1 tablespoon fresh lemon juice

Couscous Salad
4 cups cooked pearl couscous
2 cups Kentucky peas or frozen
  peas, blanched in lightly salted
  water
2 cups chopped heirloom
  tomatoes, such as Black
  Russian, Mr. Stripey, Lemon Boy
  or Ponderosa
1/4 cup mint chiffonade
1/2 cup orange juice
1 teaspoon kosher salt, or to taste
1/2 teaspoon coarse pepper

For the lamb, combine the peppercorns, salt, coriander, cinnamon, cloves, cardamom, nutmeg and paprika in a bowl. Rub 1/2 teaspoon to 2 teaspoons of the mixture over both sides of each lamb chop. Let stand for 30 to 60 minutes.

For the gastrique, combine the bourbon, blackberry purée, sorghum, bay leaf, chile flakes, sugar and salt in a saucepan and mix well. Simmer for 30 minutes, stirring occasionally.

For the syrup, combine the bourbon, chili sauce, water, sugar, garlic, sesame oil, fish sauce, tamari sauce and lemon juice in a saucepan and mix well. Simmer for 30 minutes, stirring occasionally.

For the salad, combine the couscous with the peas, tomatoes, mint, orange juice, salt and pepper in a large bowl and mix well. Keep warm or store in the refrigerator for up to 8 hours to serve cold.

To serve, preheat the grill. Grill the lamb over hot coals or on a gas grill until a meat thermometer registers 145 degrees for medium-rare. Remove to a warm plate. Reheat the gastrique and syrup over low heat. Spoon some of the syrup onto each serving plate. Discard the bay leaf in the gastrique and drip some of the gastrique into the syrup. Place 4 lamb chops on each plate and spoon the couscous salad beside the chops. Drizzle additional syrup and gastrique over the top.

*Red chili sauce is found in Asian specialty stores or the Asian section of supermarkets.

**Toasting and heating some spices in a dry hot pan and then grinding them adds flavor. You may toast the kosher salt and peppercorns for 60 seconds and heat the cinnamon, whole cloves and whole coriander seeds for 30 seconds, then grind them in a spice grinder or coffee grinder.

Pork Tenderloin with Fig Peach Chutney and Polenta

Chef Nat Tate,
Portofino Restaurant,
Lexington, Kentucky

Figs are among the most beloved fruits of the Deep South, and chutneys have graced the side tables of the region for centuries. Leave it to a young chef to add the snappy harmonies of Woodford Reserve to give this favorite a new twist.

4 servings

Fig Peach Chutney
8 ounces dried figs
1/2 cup Woodford Reserve bourbon
6 tablespoons chopped shallots
2 tablespoons olive oil
2 pounds peaches, peeled and cut into medium chunks
2/3 cup golden raisins
3/4 cup packed brown sugar
1/4 teaspoon cardamom
1/8 teaspoon ground cloves
1/2 teaspoon curry powder
1/4 teaspoon cumin
1 teaspoon salt
1/8 teaspoon cayenne pepper
1 teaspoon black pepper
6 tablespoons balsamic vinegar
5/8 cup slivered almonds, toasted

The Pork Tenderloin
1/4 cup Woodford Reserve bourbon
2 tablespoons olive oil
1 tablespoon chopped garlic
2 tablespoons chopped fresh sage
2 pounds pork tenderloin, trimmed
2 tablespoon olive oil
Creamy Polenta
4 cups water

1 cup heavy cream
4 dashes Tabasco sauce
4 dashes Worcestershire sauce
1 tablespoon finely chopped fresh rosemary
3/4 cup polenta
1/4 cup semolina flour
1 teaspoon salt
1/2 teaspoon pepper
1 cup (4 ounces) grated Parmesan cheese

For the chutney, cut the figs into halves or quarters, depending on the size. Combine with the bourbon in a bowl and let stand for 8 hours or longer. Pour into a saucepan and cover tightly. Simmer for 3 minutes or until the bourbon is absorbed.

Sauté the shallots in the heated olive oil in a sauté pan until translucent. Add the peaches and raisins and sauté for several minutes until tender. Add the brown sugar, cardamom, cloves, curry powder, cumin, salt, cayenne pepper and black pepper. Stir in the fig mixture and vinegar.

Simmer for 15 to 20 minutes or until the liquid is somewhat reduced; do not overcook, as the peaches should retain their shape. Spoon into a bowl and chill in the refrigerator. Stir in the almonds.

For the pork, combine the bourbon, 2 tablespoons olive oil, the garlic and sage in a bowl and mix well. Add the pork, coating well. Marinate in the refrigerator for 8 hours or longer, turning occasionally; drain, discarding the marinade.

Preheat the oven to 400 degrees. Heat 2 tablespoons olive oil in a large ovenproof skillet. Add the pork and sear over high heat until brown on all sides. Place in the oven and bake for 20 minutes or until a meat thermometer registers 160 degrees. Let stand for 5 to 10 minutes.

For the polenta, combine the water, cream, Tabasco sauce, Worcestershire sauce and rosemary in a saucepan and bring to a boil. Whisk in the polenta, semolina flour, salt and pepper. Reduce the heat to low and simmer for 20 minutes, stirring frequently. Remove from the heat and stir in the cheese.

To serve, spoon the polenta onto the serving plates. Slice the pork tenderloin 3/4 inch thick and arrange 4 slices around the polenta on each plate. Add a generous spoonful of the chutney to each plate.

Pork Tenderloin with Smoked Cheddar Chipotle Sweet Corn Grit Cakes

Executive Chef/Owner Anthony Lamas, Jicama Grill, Louisville, Kentucky

The smoky fire of the chipotle blends with the oaken caramel of Woodford Reserve so perfectly, you'll marvel that the chile isn't native to Kentucky. This blend of Latino and Bluegrass flavors is an inspired combo throughout.

4 servings

Adobo-Rubbed Pork Tenderloin
1/2 cup olive oil
3 tablespoons chopped garlic
1 tablespoon cumin
1 tablespoon coriander
1 tablespoon kosher salt
1 tablespoon cayenne pepper
2 pounds pork tenderloin, cut into 4 (8-ounce) portions

Chipotle-Orange Demi Sauce*
1/4 cup Woodford Reserve bourbon
1 onion, chopped
1 tablespoon chopped garlic
3 ounces chipotle chiles in adobo
1 cup crushed tomatoes
1 cup ketchup
1/2 cup rice wine vinegar
1/4 cup Worcestershire sauce
1 cup thawed frozen orange juice concentrate
1/4 cup honey
1 tablespoon paprika
1 tablespoon chili powder
1 teaspoon salt

Smoked Cheddar Chipotle Sweet Corn Grit Cakes and Assembly
3 cups water

1 tablespoon olive oil
1/4 teaspoon kosher salt
3/4 cup stone-ground grits
1/4 cup (1/2 stick) unsalted butter
11/2 tablespoons chipotle chiles in adobo
8 ounces Cheddar cheese, cut into 1-inch pieces
2/3 cup fresh Silver Queen corn kernels (about 2 ears) or frozen white Shoe Peg corn kernels
1 tablespoon olive oil
olive oil for sautéeing
flour
2 tablespoons chopped fresh cilantro

For the pork, combine the olive oil, garlic, cumin, coriander, salt and cayenne pepper in a bowl and mix well. Rub over the pork and marinate in the refrigerator for 8 hours or longer.

For the sauce, combine the bourbon, onion, garlic, chipotle chiles in adobo, tomatoes, ketchup, vinegar, Worcestershire sauce, orange juice concentrate, honey, paprika, chili powder and salt in a saucepan. Mix well and cook over medium-high heat for 5 minutes, stirring constantly. Strain through a medium mesh strainer into a bowl. Store, covered, in the refrigerator until serving time.

For the grit cakes, combine the water, 1 tablespoon olive oil and the salt in a large saucepan and bring to a boil. Add the grits and cook using the package directions, stirring in the butter and chipotle chiles in adobo as the grits begin to thicken.

94

Cook for 2 minutes longer. Add the cheese gradually and stir until melted. Stir in half the corn, reserving the remaining corn for garnish. Remove from the heat.

Grease a 12×18-inch pan with 1 tablespoon olive oil. Pour the grits into the pan and spread evenly with a rubber spatula. Place plastic wrap directly on the surface and chill for 4 to 24 hours. Cut into the desired shapes with cutters.

Preheat the oven to 350 degrees. Heat a small amount of olive oil in a sauté pan. Dust the grit cakes with flour and add to the sauté pan. Panfry for 2 minutes on each side or until golden brown. Remove to a sheet pan and bake for 3 to 5 minutes. Keep warm.

To serve, preheat the grill. Grill the pork over medium-hot coals until a meat thermometer registers 160 degrees. Reheat the sauce. Place 1 grit cake in the center of each serving plate and place 1 portion of pork next to the cake. Spoon the desired amount of sauce around the grit cake and over the pork. Garnish with the reserved corn kernels and cilantro.

*You will have extra sauce, which can be frozen to serve with other grilled beef, pork, or poultry.

Pork Chops with Green Tomato and Mango Relish

Culinary Director/Owner Jim Gerhardt, Limestone Restaurant, Louisville, Kentucky

4 servings

Green Tomato and Mango Relish
juice of 1 small lime
1 tablespoon honey
2 tablespoons chopped fresh cilantro
1/2 teaspoon cumin
1 green tomato, peeled and seeded
1 mango
1/2 roasted red bell pepper
1/2 small red onion
kosher salt or sea salt to taste
Fried Plantain (optional)
1 cup peanut oil, corn oil or safflower oil for deep-frying
1 large plantain, cut into 1/8-inch slices

The Pork Chops
2 tablespoons Woodford Reserve bourbon
1/4 cup maple syrup
1/4 cup Kentucky sorghum molasses
2 tablespoons sweet chili sauce*
1 1/2 teaspoons garlic chili paste*
4 (4-ounce) Frenched center-cut rib pork chops

Country Ham Jus
8 ounces Kentucky country ham bones or smoked pork hocks
4 cups water
1 small onion, chopped
1 rib celery, chopped
1 small carrot, chopped
1 sprig of fresh thyme, or 1/2 teaspoon dried thyme
1 bay leaf

1 tablespoon whole peppercorns
2 cups demi-glace or very rich veal stock**
kosher salt or sea salt to taste

For the relish, combine the lime juice, honey, cilantro and cumin in a bowl and mix well. Cut the green tomato, mango, bell pepper and onion into 1/4-inch pieces. Add to the lime juice mixture. Season to taste with salt and toss to mix well. Let stand at room temperature for 30 minutes or store, tightly covered, in the refrigerator for 8 hours or longer.

For the plantain, heat the peanut oil to 350 degrees in a deep skillet. Add the plantain and deep-fry until light brown; drain on paper towels. Let stand, uncovered, for 8 hours or longer to crisp. You may prepare them at serving time and serve warm if preferred.

For the pork chops, combine the bourbon, maple syrup, molasses, chili sauce and chili paste in a bowl and mix well. Add the pork chops, turning to coat well. Marinate, covered, in the refrigerator for 8 hours or longer.

For the country ham jus, combine the ham bones, water, onion, celery, carrot, thyme, bay leaf and peppercorns in a large stockpot. Simmer, uncovered, for 3 hours or until reduced to 1 cup. Strain through a medium mesh strainer. Combine with the demi-glace in a

saucepan and mix well. Cook until reduced by 1/2, stirring frequently. Season to taste with salt and store, covered, in the refrigerator for up to 2 days.

To serve, preheat the grill. Drain the pork chops, discarding the marinade, and insert a meat thermometer into the thickest portion of 1 chop without touching the bone. Grill over medium-hot coals for 10 minutes on each side or until a meat thermometer registers 160 degrees; the juices should run clear when the centers of the chops are pressed. Reheat the country ham jus and spoon 1/4 cup onto each serving plate. Place the pork chops on the plates and add a generous spoonful of the relish. Top with 2 slices of fried plantain if desired.

*Sweet chili sauce and garlic chili paste can be found in the Asian section of most supermarkets.

**Demi-glace is sold in small packages at specialty supermarkets, usually near the butcher's counter.

Woodford Steak Salad

David Larson, Chef-in-Residence, Woodford Reserve Distillery, Versailles, Kentucky

6 servings

The Steak
1 tablespoon Woodford Reserve bourbon
1/2 cup olive oil
1 tablespoon soy sauce
2 tablespoons ketchup
1/2 teaspoon salt
1 teaspoon pepper
2 pounds top sirloin steak

The Vegetables
6 new potatoes
salt to taste
1/2 cup cherry tomatoes, cut into halves
2 medium carrots, thinly sliced on the diagonal
1 small zucchini, julienned
1/3 cup thin red bell pepper strips
1/3 cup finely chopped scallions
1/2 cup broccoli florets

Basil Vinaigrette
1/2 cup olive oil
2 tablespoons balsamic vinegar
1 teaspoon Dijon mustard
2 tablespoons finely chopped fresh basil
2 tablespoons finely chopped fresh Italian parsley
1 tablespoon capers
1/16 teaspoon sugar
1/2 teaspoon salt
1/2 teaspoon pepper

For the steak, combine the bourbon, olive oil, soy sauce, ketchup, salt and pepper in a shallow dish and mix well. Add the steak and turn to coat well. Marinate in the refrigerator for 45 minutes, turning occasionally; drain, discarding the marinade.

Preheat the grill. Grill the steak until a meat thermometer registers 145 degrees for medium-rare. Let stand until cool and cut into bite-size strips.

For the vegetables, cook the potatoes in boiling salted water in a saucepan until tender. Drain, cool and cut into quarters. Combine with the tomatoes, carrots, zucchini, bell pepper, scallions, broccoli and steak in a large salad bowl and mix gently.

For the vinaigrette, whisk the olive oil, vinegar, Dijon mustard, basil, parsley, capers, sugar, salt and pepper in a bowl. Add the vinaigrette to the steak and vegetable mixture and toss to coat. Serve from the bowl or spoon onto a serving platter.

Tournedos Rossini

Chef/Owner Dean Corbett and Executive Chef David Cuntz, Equus Restaurant, Louisville, Kentucky

A tournedo is a medallion cut from the tenderloin of beef, about 3/4 to 1 inch thick and 2 to 2 1/2 inches in diameter. The inspired team of Equus chefs have used Woodford Reserve to create a tournedos dish that is a cut above all the rest.

2 servings

2 (8-ounce) prime beef tenderloin fillets
salt and pepper to taste
1 tablespoon butter
1 teaspoon butter
1/4 teaspoon chopped garlic
1 teaspoon chopped shallot
1 tablespoon tomato purée
1/4 cup Woodford Reserve bourbon
1/2 teaspoon chopped fresh rosemary
8 ounces demi-glace or rich veal stock*
2 tablespoons butter
3/4 cup sliced cremini or shiitake mushrooms
4 slices pâté de fois gras studded with black truffle

Cut the beef medallions into halves to form 4 tournedos 3/4 to 1 inch thick and 2 to 21/2 inches in diameter. Season the tournedos to taste with salt and pepper. Melt 1 tablespoon butter in a heavy sauté pan. Add the beef and sauté for 3 minutes on each side for medium-rare, or until a meat thermometer registers 145 degrees. Remove from the pan and keep warm.

Melt 1 teaspoon butter in the same sauté pan and add the garlic, shallot, tomato purée, bourbon and rosemary. Bring to a simmer, stirring to mix well. Remove from the heat. Ignite the mixture with a long-handled lighter and allow the flames to subside; most of the liquid should evaporate. Add the demi-glace and return to the heat. Cook until reduced to the desired consistency. Melt 2 tablespoons butter in a clean sauté pan and add the mushrooms. Sauté over medium heat for 5 minutes or until light brown.

To serve, place 2 tournedos on each plate and top each with a slice of pâté. Spoon the mushrooms and bourbon sauce over the top and serve immediately.

*Demi-glace is sold in small packages at specialty supermarkets, usually near the butcher counter.

Demi-Glace

David Larson, Chef-in-Residence, Woodford Reserve Distillery, Versailles, Kentucky

Makes about 2 cups

2 tablespoons unsalted butter
2 onions, chopped
2 large carrots, chopped
1 tablespoon sugar
3 tablespoons flour
2 cups low-salt beef broth
1 cup low-salt chicken broth
1 tablespoon tomato paste
2 garlic cloves, minced
    bouquet garni*
1/2 teaspoon salt
1/2 teaspoon freshly ground
    pepper
2 tablespoons Woodford Reserve
    bourbon
1 tablespoon Madeira or cream
    sherry
browning sauce (optional)

Melt the butter in a heavy saucepan over medium heat. Add the onions and carrots and cook for 20 minutes, stirring frequently. Stir in the sugar and increase the heat. Cook for 10 minutes or until the vegetables are caramelized, stirring constantly to prevent burning; the vegetables will add a brown color to the sauce.

Stir in the flour. Cook for 3 minutes or until the flour is golden brown, stirring constantly. Stir in the beef broth, chicken broth, tomato paste, garlic, bouquet garni, salt and pepper. Bring to a boil, stirring constantly. Reduce the heat and simmer, loosely covered, for 1 hour, stirring occasionally.

Add the bourbon and wine and discard the bouquet garni. You can add a few drops of browning sauce for a darker brown color. Freeze for future use if desired.

*To make a **Bouquet Garni**, combine a small bunch of parsley, 8 sprigs of fresh thyme or 1 teaspoon dried thyme, 1 bay leaf and 2 or 3 celery leaves on a 4×4-inch square of cheesecloth. Tie the cheesecloth to enclose the herbs and add to the sauce. You can substitute dried herbs for fresh herbs, adding them directly to the sauce.

Kentucky Bourbon Grilling Sauce

Chef Mark Williams, Brown-Forman Corporation, Louisville, Kentucky

Makes 3 cups

1 cup ketchup
1/2 cup apple cider vinegar
1/4 cup peanut oil
1/2 cup fresh lemon juice
1/4 cup honey
1/4 cup soy sauce
1/2 cup packed brown sugar
1/4 cup whole grain mustard
1/2 cup finely chopped sweet
    onion
1/4 cup finely chopped garlic
1/4 cup finely chopped fresh
    gingerroot
1/4 cup finely chopped fresh
    rosemary
1 teaspoon red pepper flakes
1 tablespoon liquid smoke
1/4 cup Woodford Reserve
    bourbon

Combine the ketchup, vinegar, peanut oil, lemon juice, honey and soy sauce in a saucepan and mix well. Stir in the brown sugar, whole grain mustard, onion, garlic, gingerroot, rosemary, red pepper flakes and liquid smoke. Simmer for 10 minutes, stirring occasionally. Remove from the heat and stir in the bourbon.

You may thin the sauce with water to use as a marinade for grilled meats if desired.

"Then I discovered Woodford Reserve, which has that same nice oak-y, smoky, earthy aroma, but also some sweetness that makes it even more versatile."

Chef Peng S. Looi

97

Poached Chicken Salad with Cherries and Nectarines

Mary Ann Thoren,
Woodford Reserve's kitchen

This is not your traditional chicken salad, but we bet you will love it. Very nice served with yeast rolls hot from the oven.

4 servings

The Salad
3 cups water
1 cup Woodford Reserve bourbon
2 carrots, cut into halves
2 ribs celery, cut into halves
1 onion, cut into quarters
8 boneless skinless chicken
    breasts
2 cups pitted sweet cherries
2 cups sliced peeled nectarines
1 cup chopped celery
1/4 cup pecans or almonds,
    toasted and chopped
11/2 teaspoons fresh lemon juice

Ginger Curry Dressing and
Assembly
1 cup mayonnaise
1/2 cup sour cream
1/4 cup finely chopped onion
1 tablespoon chopped preserved
    ginger
11/2 teaspoons salt
3/4 teaspoon curry powder
lettuce leaves

For the salad, bring the water, bourbon, carrots, celery halves and onion to a boil in a large saucepan. Add the chicken and reduce the heat to low. Poach the chicken for 15 to 18 minutes or until cooked through.

Drain and cool slightly, discarding the solids. Chop the chicken into bite-size pieces and mix with the cherries, nectarines, chopped celery, almonds and lemon juice in a bowl.

For the dressing, combine the mayonnaise, sour cream, onion, ginger, salt and curry powder in a bowl and mix well. Add the dressing to the salad mixture and stir until coated. Spoon the chicken salad onto lettuce-lined serving plates and serve immediately or chill, covered, until serving time.

Scale House Pasta with Chargrilled Chicken Breasts

David Larson, Chef-in-Residence, Woodford Reserve Distillery, Versailles, Kentucky

So simple to throw together, but so full of textures and flavors! This will become a regular part of your cooking repertoire.

4 servings

3 tablespoons butter
8 ounces mushrooms, sliced
1 red bell pepper, chopped
1/4 cup Woodford Reserve bourbon
1 pound boneless skinless chicken breasts, chargrilled and cut into strips
8 ounces penne, cooked al dente and drained
3/4 cup heavy cream
2 tablespoons chopped fresh parsley
1 tablespoon chopped fresh thyme
1 tablespoon chopped fresh oregano
3 tablespoons grated Romano cheese
salt and pepper to taste

Heat a large sauté pan over medium heat and add the butter. Sauté the mushrooms in the butter for 2 minutes. Stir in the bell pepper and sauté for 2 minutes longer. Mix in the bourbon. Reduce the heat to low.

Simmer for 5 minutes, stirring occasionally. Stir in the chicken, pasta, heavy cream, parsley, thyme and oregano. Simmer for 2 minutes longer, stirring occasionally. Add the cheese, salt and pepper and mix well. Spoon the pasta mixture onto 4 serving plates and serve immediately.

Southern Chicken Hash Patties with Dried Cherry and Bourbon Sauce

Chef Brian C. Jennings,
Hyatt Regency,
Lexington, Kentucky

Yes, this looks like a very complex recipe, but if you take it in simple steps, it's quite easy to prepare, and the result is divine in both presentation and flavor. If you like, you can make the hash patties the day before you wish to serve and refrigerate.

4 servings

Chicken Hash Patties
2 Granny Smith apples, peeled
   and cut into quarters
4 (6-ounce) boneless skinless
   chicken breasts
1/4 cup Woodford Reserve
   bourbon
1 sprig of fresh thyme
1 teaspoon kosher salt
1/2 teaspoon cracked black pepper
1 tablespoon olive oil
6 tablespoons heavy cream

Squash Haystacks
julienned peel of 1 small zucchini
julienned peel of 1 small yellow
   squash
1/2 red bell pepper, finely julienned
salt and pepper to taste

Country Ham Cracklings
2 ounces Kentucky country ham,
   finely julienned
vegetable oil for frying

**Dried Cherry and Bourbon Sauce
and Assembly**
15 dried cherries
1/4 cup Woodford Reserve
   bourbon

1/2 cup homemade or canned
   chicken stock
1 tablespoon brown sugar
juice of 1 orange
1/4 cup (1/2 stick) butter, chilled and
   cut into 1/2-inch chunks
1/16 teaspoon salt
4 tablespoons olive oil
1/4 cup panko
1 tablespoon butter
4 fresh basil leaves
sections of 1 orange

For the hash, preheat the oven to 350 degrees. Arrange the apples in a baking dish and bake for 20 minutes or until tender; maintain the oven temperature. Cool the apples and cut into 1/2-inch pieces. Place 3 of the chicken breasts in a nonreactive dish. Whisk the bourbon, thyme, 1/2 teaspoon of the salt, 1/4 teaspoon of the pepper and the olive oil in a bowl and drizzle over the chicken, turning to coat. Marinate, covered, in the refrigerator for 15 to 20 minutes. Cut the remaining chicken breast into 6 portions and process in a food processor with the remaining 1/2 teaspoon salt and remaining 1/4 teaspoon pepper until chopped. Add the heavy cream gradually, processing constantly until incorporated. Chill, covered, in the refrigerator.

   For the haystacks, mix the zucchini peel, yellow squash peel, bell pepper, salt and pepper in a bowl.

   For the cracklings, fry the ham in oil in a skillet for 1 minute or until crisp. Drain on paper towels and set aside.

For the sauce, soak the cherries in the bourbon in a bowl for 1 hour or longer. Combine the undrained cherries, stock, brown sugar and orange juice in an 8-inch sauté pan. Cook over medium heat until the mixture is reduced and of a sauce consistency, stirring frequently. Whisk in 1/4 cup butter and the salt. Remove from the heat and cover to keep warm.

Heat 2 tablespoons of the olive oil in a 12-inch sauté pan over medium-high heat. Sear the marinated chicken in the hot oil for 20 to 30 seconds per side. Cool slightly and cut into 1/2-inch pieces. Fold the chopped chicken and apples into the chilled cream mixture. Shape the chicken mixture into four 3-inch round patties. You may prepare to this point up to 24 hours in advance and store, covered, in the refrigerator.

Mix 1 tablespoon of the olive oil and the bread crumbs in a shallow dish and lightly coat each patty. Sauté the patties in a mixture of the remaining 1 tablespoon olive oil and 1 tablespoon butter in a sauté pan over medium-high heat for 2 minutes per side or until golden brown. Arrange the patties in a greased baking dish and bake for 15 minutes or until a meat thermometer registers 170 degrees. Let rest for 2 to 3 minutes.

To serve, arrange 1 patty on each of 4 serving plates. Drizzle the warm sauce around the outer edge of each plate. Top each patty with some of the squash mixture, using the tines of a fork to make it resemble a haystack. Sprinkle each serving with 1 basil leaf, some of the cracklings and some of the orange sections. Serve immediately.

Lettuce Wraps

Executive Chef John Castro, Winston's Restaurant, Louisville, Kentucky

These wraps make for an informal and delightfully messy summer supper. Complete the meal with a rice salad from the deli (adding chopped bell peppers and a splash of rice vinegar if desired) and ice cream sprinkled with minced crystallized ginger.

Makes 6 wraps

1 tablespoon peanut oil
1 large onion, chopped
11/4 pounds boneless skinless chicken breasts, cut into bite size pieces
1/2 cup Asian peanut sauce
1 tablespoon hoisin sauce
1 tablespoon soy sauce
1 cucumber, peeled, seeded and chopped (about 11/4 cups)
1/3 cup coarsely chopped fresh mint
1/2 cup fresh cilantro sprigs
1/3 cup peanuts, coarsely chopped
1/4 cup lime juice
1/4 cup finely shredded fresh coconut or unsweetened shredded coconut
2 tablespoons minced fresh lemon grass
1 tablespoon (or more) Woodford Reserve bourbon
salt and pepper to taste
6 large butter lettuce or iceberg lettuce leaves
1/3 cup fresh cilantro sprigs
1/3 cup small fresh mint sprigs

Heat the peanut oil in a large heavy skillet over medium-high heat. Sauté the onion in the hot oil for 3 minutes or until the onion begins to brown. Stir in the chicken and sauté for 7 minutes or until brown and cooked through. Add the peanut sauce, hoisin sauce and soy sauce and cook until heated through, stirring occasionally. Stir in the cucumber, chopped mint, 1/2 cup cilantro, the peanuts, lime juice, coconut, lemon grass and bourbon. Season to taste with salt and pepper.

Spoon the chicken mixture into a medium bowl and place in the middle of a serving platter. Surround the bowl with the lettuce leaves, 1/3 cup cilantro and the mint sprigs. Instruct guests to spoon some of the chicken mixture onto each lettuce leaf and sprinkle with a few sprigs of cilantro and mint. Fold the sides over the filling and roll to enclose. Pass with additional soy sauce for dipping.

Molasses-Marinated Breast of Duck

*Chef Marcus John Heindselman,
Louisville Country Club,
Louisville, Kentucky*

*Sous Chef Marcus Heindselman
likes to serve this succulent duck
with his Whipped Potatoes and
Haricots Verts with Toasted
Almonds. You should be able to
find duck breast at many
markets or specialty butcher
shops, but if not, pork loin is also
stunningly good.*

4 servings

Apple Ginger Chutney
3/4 cup finely chopped yellow
   onion
2 tablespoons butter
2 Granny Smith apples, peeled
   and finely chopped
1 cup packed brown sugar
1/2 cup currants
1/2 cup apple cider vinegar
1/4 cup finely chopped fresh
   gingerroot

The Duck
3/4 cup molasses
1/2 cup Woodford Reserve
   bourbon
2 tablespoons Worcestershire
   sauce
4 duck breasts

Whipped Potatoes
6 medium russet potatoes, peeled,
   cut into quarters and cooked
1/2 cup milk
1/4 cup (1/2 stick) butter, softened
6 ounces cream cheese, softened
1/2 teaspoon salt
1/8 teaspoon white pepper

**Haricots Verts with Toasted
Almonds and Assembly**
2 cups water
2 tablespoons kosher salt
1/16 teaspoon baking soda
6 ounces haricots verts, trimmed
1 tablespoon butter
1 ounce slivered almonds
1 tablespoon chopped shallots
1 teaspoon chopped garlic
salt and pepper to taste

For the chutney, sauté the onion in the butter in a sauté pan until tender. Stir in the apples, brown sugar, currants, vinegar and gingerroot and cook for 20 minutes or until the apples are tender and the liquid has reduced, stirring frequently. Process 1/2 of the apple mixture in a blender or food processor until puréed. Return the purée to the sauté pan and mix well. Let stand until cool. You may prepare up to 2 days in advance and store, covered, in the refrigerator.

For the duck, whisk the molasses, bourbon and Worcestershire sauce in a bowl. Lightly score the fat diagonally on the duck with a sharp knife and arrange the duck in a shallow dish. Pour the molasses mixture over the duck, turning to coat. Marinate, covered, in the refrigerator for 8 to 10 hours, turning occasionally.

Preheat the grill. Drain the duck, discarding the marinade, and grill over hot coals until a meat thermometer registers 180 degrees.

Let rest for 15 minutes and slice each breast into 4 equal portions. You may substitute 2 pounds trimmed pork tenderloin cut into four 8-ounce portions for the duck.

For the potatoes, beat the potatoes, milk, butter, cream cheese, salt and white pepper in a mixing bowl until light and fluffy. Cover to keep warm. You may prepare up to 1 day in advance and store, covered, in the refrigerator. Reheat at 350 degrees for 30 minutes or until heated through.

For the haricots verts, bring the water, 2 tablespoons salt and baking soda to a boil in a large saucepan and add the haricots verts. Cook for 5 minutes. Drain in a colander and rinse with cold water. Heat the butter in a sauté pan over medium heat until brown. Stir in the almonds, shallots and garlic and sauté until light brown. Add the haricots verts, salt to taste and pepper and stir until coated.

To serve, mound 1/4 of the potatoes in the center of each of 4 serving plates. Arrange 4 slices of the duck around each serving of potatoes and top with a generous spoonful of the chutney. Spoon the haricots verts on the sides of the plates.

Many bourbons tend to fall squarely into the sweet or savory camp, but Jim notes that "Woodford Reserve is an exception in that it works both ways."

Chef Jim Gerhardt

Rod's favorite creation is a cocktail with Woodford Reserve, blackberries, peaches, and some simple syrup. "I think it's better than sangria."

Chef Rod Jones

Smoked Turkey and Swiss Sandwiches

Chef Mark Williams, Brown-Forman Corporation, Louisville, Kentucky

You may think you know about turkey and cheese sandwiches, but this delectable grilled creation with bourbon chutney zing will give you a whole new perspective. You may also wish to eliminate the grilling and serve the sandwiches cold, dressed with sliced tomatoes in season and green leaf lettuce.

Makes 2 sandwiches

1/4 **cup chutney**
2 **tablespoons Woodford Reserve bourbon**
8 **ounces smoked turkey, thinly sliced**
4 **ounces Swiss cheese, thinly sliced**
2 **ounces thinly sliced red onion**
4 **slices whole wheat bread**
1/4 **cup (**1/2 **stick) butter, softened**

Mix the chutney and bourbon in a bowl. Layer the turkey, cheese and onion equally on 2 slices of the bread. Spread the chutney mixture on 1 side of each of the remaining 2 slices of bread and arrange the slices chutney side down over the prepared layers.

Spread the sandwiches with the butter and grill on a griddle or in a skillet until the cheese melts and the bread is golden brown.

Mustard Seed-Crusted Alaskan Wild King Salmon

Craig Thompson, Former Chef at Harper's Restaurant, Louisville, Kentucky

4 servings

Sweet Potato Purée
2 large sweet potatoes
1/2 cup heavy cream
1/2 cup packed brown sugar
1/2 cup dark corn syrup
1/4 cup (1/2 stick) butter
2 tablespoons water
1/4 cup apple cider vinegar
1/4 cup Woodford Reserve
    bourbon
1 tablespoon chopped shallots
1 teaspoon salt
1/2 teaspoon cracked black pepper
1/8 teaspoon allspice

Honey Ginger Glaze
1/2 cup honey
2 tablespoons grated fresh
    gingerroot
2 garlic cloves, minced
2 tablespoons Woodford Reserve
    bourbon
1 teaspoon white truffle oil

Swiss Chard
1 tablespoon olive oil
1/4 cup chopped applewood
    smoked bacon
1 onion, chopped
1/2 fennel bulb, chopped
1 garlic clove, minced
1 tablespoon chopped shallots
1 pound Swiss chard, trimmed and
    chopped

The Salmon
2 tablespoons red mustard seeds
2 tablespoons yellow mustard
    seeds

1 tablespoon poppy seeds
2 pounds Alaskan wild king
    salmon, skin removed
2 tablespoons olive oil

For the purée, preheat the oven to 425 degrees. Pierce the sweet potatoes with a fork and arrange on a baking sheet. Bake for 30 minutes and reduce the heat to 375 degrees. Bake for 45 minutes longer or until tender. Let stand just until cool enough to handle. Peel and cut into chunks. Bring the heavy cream to a simmer in a saucepan and remove from the heat. Bring the brown sugar, corn syrup, butter and water to a boil in a medium saucepan, stirring occasionally. Boil for 1 minute and stir in the hot cream. Boil for 1 minute longer. Remove from the heat and cool slightly.

Process the sweet potatoes, warm cream mixture, vinegar, bourbon, shallots, salt, pepper and allspice in a food processor for 30 seconds or until puréed. Return the purée to the saucepan and cover to keep warm.

For the glaze, mix the honey, gingerroot, garlic, bourbon and truffle oil in a bowl and set aside.

For the chard, heat the olive oil in a medium sauté pan over medium-high heat. Add the bacon and sauté until crisp. Drain on paper towels, reserving the pan drippings. Crumble the bacon. Cook the onion, fennel, garlic and shallots in the reserved pan drippings for 5 minutes or until the onion is tender, stirring frequently. Add the chard and bacon to the onion mixture and sauté for 5 minutes or until the chard is tender. Remove from the heat and cover to keep warm.

For the salmon, preheat the oven to 375 degrees. Mix the mustard seeds and poppy seeds in a bowl and pat the mustard seed mixture over the top of the fillets. Heat the olive oil in a medium sauté pan over medium-high heat. Add the fillets crust side down to the hot oil and sauté for 3 minutes. Turn and sauté for 2 minutes longer. Arrange the fillets on a baking sheet and drizzle with 1 tablespoon of the glaze. Bake for 5 minutes or to the desired degree of doneness.

To serve, spread the warm potato purée evenly on each of 4 serving plates and top each serving with 1/4 of the chard and 1 salmon fillet. Drizzle with the remaining glaze and serve immediately.

"I was so excited when I saw the Flavor Wheel. It's such a great concept!"

Chef John Castro

Pecan-Crusted Red Snapper

Executive Chef David Cuntz, Equus Restaurant, Louisville, Kentucky

This elegant dish is a snap to make, especially if you prepare the sauce a day in advance, refrigerate, and reheat over low heat before serving. The fish pairs well with a simple accompaniment of wild rice and grilled vegetables.

4 servings

The Snapper
2 cups pecans, finely chopped
1/2 cup packed brown sugar
salt and pepper to taste
4 (8-ounce) red snapper fillets

Bourbon Sauce and Assembly
1 tablespoon chopped shallots
1 tablespoon chopped garlic
1 tablespoon butter
1 cup Woodford Reserve bourbon
1/2 cup honey
juice and grated zest of 1 lemon
1/2 cup (1 stick) butter, chilled and
   cut into 1/2-inch cubes
salt and pepper to taste
chopped fresh parsley

For the snapper, preheat the oven to 400 degrees. Mix the pecans, brown sugar, salt and pepper in a shallow dish. Coat the fillets evenly with the pecan mixture and arrange in a single layer in a baking dish sprayed with nonstick cooking spray. Bake for 8 to 10 minutes or approximately 10 minutes per inch of thickness.

For the sauce, cook the shallots and garlic in 1 tablespoon butter in a medium saucepan until tender but not brown. Deglaze the pan with the bourbon. Cook over medium-high heat until the liquid is reduced by 1/2, stirring frequently. Stir in the honey, lemon juice and lemon zest.

Bring to a boil and reduce the heat. Simmer for 2 minutes, stirring frequently. Remove from the heat and whisk in 1/2 cup butter until blended. Season to taste with salt and pepper. Drizzle the sauce over the fillets on serving plates and sprinkle with parsley. Serve with wild rice and grilled vegetables. You may prepare the sauce up to 24 hours in advance and store, covered, in the refrigerator. Reheat over low heat.

Seared Scallops with Sweet Corn Polenta

*Chef/Owner Ouita Michel,
Holly Hill Inn,
Midway, Kentucky*

The sweethearts of the sea meet the sweetness of fine bourbon for a blissful marriage of taste. This dish is particularly fine when you use Weisenberger grits and Kenny's Country cheese, both up the road from Holly Hill.

4 servings

Sweet Corn Polenta
3 cups water
1 cup stone-ground yellow grits
1 teaspoon salt
1/2 cup (2 ounces) shredded Jarlsberg cheese
2 tablespoons butter
    kernels of 2 ears fresh or frozen corn
salt and pepper to taste

Scallops and Assembly
1 1/2 pounds dry-pack large sea scallops*
salt and ground white pepper to taste
2 tablespoons clarified butter**
2 shallots, thinly sliced
2 garlic cloves, minced
1 cup Woodford Reserve bourbon
1/2 cup seafood stock
1 cup crème fraîche (page 91)
16 cherry tomatoes
2 tablespoons coarsely chopped fresh tarragon
fresh tarragon leaves or chives

For the polenta, bring the water to a boil in a heavy saucepan over high heat. Gradually sprinkle the grits over the boiling water, stirring constantly with a wooden spoon. Stir in 1 teaspoon salt and reduce the heat to low. Cook for 30 minutes and stir in the cheese and butter. Taste and adjust the seasonings. The polenta should be the consistency of soft whipped potatoes. If too thick, add milk, and if too thin, cook a little longer or sprinkle in a small amount of grits. Stir in the corn and season to taste with salt and pepper just before serving.

For the scallops, pat the scallops with paper towels and season to taste with salt and white pepper. Heat a sauté pan until hot and add the clarified butter. Sear the scallops in the hot butter for 2 minutes. Turn and sear for 1 minute longer or until they are no longer translucent; do not overcook. Remove from the heat and cover to keep warm, reserving the pan juices.

Add the shallots, garlic and bourbon to the reserved pan juices and cook over medium heat until heated through, stirring frequently. Remove from the heat and carefully ignite with a long-handled lighter. Let the flames subside and return the sauté pan to the stove-top.

Cook over medium-high heat until the mixture is reduced to 3 tablespoons, stirring frequently. Stir in the stock and cook until the mixture is reduced to 1/2 cup, stirring frequently.

Stir in the crème fraîche, tomatoes and chopped tarragon. Taste and season with salt. Cook until heated through and stir in the scallops.

To serve, mound 1/4 of the polenta in the center of each of 4 serving plates. Arrange the scallops and tomatoes around the polenta and drizzle with the sauce. Garnish with tarragon leaves.

*It is important to purchase dry-pack scallops; otherwise, the liquid will release from the scallops and they will not brown.

For **Clarified Butter, slowly melt unsalted butter in a sauté pan. Skim the foam off the top and pour the clear liquid off and use as clarified butter. Discard the milky solids that collect in the bottom of the saucepan.

Grilled Shrimp with Country Ham and Goat Cheese Grits

*Chef Patrick Colley,
Louisville Country Club,
Louisville, Kentucky*

Shrimp and grits is cooking from the South Carolina Low Country at its finest. Now, Patrick Colley adds fine bourbon and goat cheese to make a good thing even better.

4 servings

Country Ham Gravy
2 tablespoons unsalted butter
2 tablespoons finely chopped celery
2 tablespoons finely minced shallots
1/2 cup sliced shiitake mushrooms
1/2 cup finely chopped country ham
2 tablespoons unsalted butter
1/4 cup flour
2 cups chicken broth
1/4 cup Woodford Reserve bourbon
salt and coarsely ground pepper to taste

Goat Cheese Grits
1 1/2 cups chicken broth
1 1/2 cups heavy cream
2 tablespoons finely minced garlic
1/2 teaspoon kosher salt
1 cup stone-ground white grits
1/2 cup fresh corn kernels (about 1 ear)
1/4 cup fresh spinach, julienned
2 ounces goat cheese, crumbled
kosher salt and coarsely ground pepper to taste

The Shrimp
1 pound medium (26- to 30-count) shrimp, peeled and deveined
1/4 cup Woodford Reserve bourbon
1/4 cup olive oil
2 teaspoons sugar
1 teaspoon kosher salt
1 teaspoon chili powder
1 teaspoon paprika
1 teaspoon granulated garlic
1/2 teaspoon cayenne pepper
1/2 teaspoon thyme
1/2 teaspoon coarsely ground black pepper
1/2 teaspoon dry mustard
1/4 teaspoon coriander
minced zest of 1/2 lime
2 to 3 tablespoons chopped fresh parsley

For the gravy, heat 2 tablespoons butter in a medium saucepan over medium heat. Add the celery and shallots and cook for 5 minutes or until tender, stirring occasionally. Stir in the mushrooms and cook until tender, stirring occasionally. Add the ham and cook for 1 minute longer, stirring occasionally. Stir in 2 tablespoons butter and reduce the heat to low.

Cook until the butter melts, stirring constantly. Add the flour gradually and cook for 1 minute, stirring constantly. The mixture will have a pasty consistency. Stir in 1 cup of the broth and cook until thickened, stirring constantly. Remove from the heat and stir in the bourbon and remaining 1 cup broth. Return to the heat and bring to a boil over medium-high heat. Reduce the heat to low and simmer for 15 minutes, stirring occasionally. Season to taste with salt and pepper and cover to keep warm. The type of country ham used will determine the quantity of salt added.

For the grits, bring the broth, heavy cream, garlic and salt to a boil in a saucepan over medium-high heat. Gradually whisk the grits into the broth mixture and reduce the heat to medium-low. Cook for 10 minutes and stir in the corn, stirring occasionally. Cook for 5 minutes and reduce the heat to low. Stir in the spinach and cheese.

Season to taste with salt and pepper and cover to keep warm. The grits should be creamy. Add additional cream, additional broth or water if the grits become too thick after standing.

For the shrimp, soak 4 bamboo skewers in water for 30 minutes. Preheat the grill to medium-high. Toss the shrimp, bourbon and olive oil in a bowl. Mix the sugar, salt, chili powder, paprika, garlic, cayenne pepper, thyme, black pepper, dry mustard, coriander and lime zest in a bowl and add to the shrimp mixture, stirring until coated.

Arrange 6 of the shrimp on a flat surface in the "C" position. Gently thread 1 of the skewers through the shrimp, making sure to maintain the "C" shape. Repeat the process with the remaining shrimp and remaining skewers. Arrange the skewers on the hot grill rack and grill for 1 to 2 minutes per side or until the shrimp turn pink, turning once.

To serve, mound 1/4 of the grits in each of 4 large serving bowls. Remove the shrimp from the skewers and arrange 6 shrimp around each mound of grits. Drizzle each serving with 3 to 4 ounces of the gravy and sprinkle with the parsley.

Rolled Cheese Soufflé with Pepper Sauce

David Larson, Chef-in-Residence, Woodford Reserve Distillery, Versailles, Kentucky

Here's a savory supper that pays homage to that other Versailles, but with a Kentucky accent.

8 servings

White Sauce
1/4 cup (1/2 stick) butter
1/4 cup flour
21/4 cups half-and-half
1 teaspoon salt
1/4 teaspoon cayenne pepper
Spinach and Shrimp Filling
2 tablespoons butter
10 ounces fresh baby spinach, trimmed
1/4 cup minced shallots
11/2 cups julienned red bell peppers
2 garlic cloves, chopped
12 ounces medium (26- to 30 count) shrimp, peeled, deveined and cut into bite-size pieces
2 tablespoons Woodford Reserve bourbon
1/4 teaspoon salt

Red Bell Pepper Sauce
1 tablespoon butter
2 tablespoons chopped onion
1/2 teaspoon chopped garlic
3 red bell peppers, chopped
3/4 cup rich chicken stock
2 tablespoons butter
11/2 tablespoons flour
1 teaspoon lemon juice
1/2 teaspoon salt
1/4 teaspoon freshly ground pepper

Soufflé
2 tablespoons grated Parmesan cheese
10 egg yolks
10 egg whites
11/4 cups (5 ounces) grated Gruyère cheese
6 tablespoons grated Parmesan cheese
salt and white pepper to taste

For the white sauce, melt the butter in a saucepan. Add the flour and cook for 1 minute, stirring constantly. Add the half-and-half gradually and cook over medium heat until thickened, stirring constantly. Stir in the salt and cayenne pepper.

For the filling, melt 1 tablespoon of the butter in a large sauté pan. Sauté the spinach and shallots in the butter until tender. Press the excess moisture from the spinach mixture and combine with 1/2 cup of the white sauce in a bowl.

Sauté the bell peppers and garlic in the remaining 1 tablespoon butter in a large sauté pan just until the bell peppers begin to soften. Stir in the shrimp and cook for 2 to 3 minutes or until the shrimp are pink and cooked through; drain. Add the bourbon and cook until the liquid evaporates. Stir in the salt and combine with the spinach mixture. Cool slightly and chill, covered, in the refrigerator. You may prepare up to 1 day in advance and store, covered, in the refrigerator.

For the bell pepper sauce, melt 1 tablespoon butter in a saucepan. Add the onion and garlic and cook for 1 minute, stirring occasionally. Add the bell peppers and stir until coated. Stir in the stock and simmer for 25 minutes or until the bell peppers are tender, stirring occasionally. Cool slightly.

Process the bell pepper mixture in a food processor until puréed and strain, discarding the solids. Mix 2 tablespoons butter and the flour in a bowl until of a pasty consistency. Combine the purée and flour mixture in the saucepan and cook until smooth and thickened, stirring frequently. Add the lemon juice, salt and pepper and mix well.

For the soufflé, preheat the oven to 425 degrees. Lightly butter an 11×17-inch baking pan and line with baking parchment. Brush the parchment with butter and sprinkle with 2 tablespoons Parmesan cheese. Whisk the egg yolks and 2 cups of the white sauce in a bowl until blended.

Beat the egg whites in a mixing bowl until soft peaks form. Fold a small portion of the egg whites into the egg yolk mixture to lighten. Fold in the remaining egg whites, Gruyère cheese and 6 tablespoons Parmesan cheese; do not overmix. Season to taste with salt and white pepper and spread in the prepared pan. Bake for 12 minutes or until

brown and puffy. Cool in the pan on a wire rack for 10 minutes.

Invert the slightly cooled soufflé onto a buttered sheet of foil. Spread the filling evenly over the soufflé, roll as for a jelly roll and wrap tightly in foil. Slice and serve at this point or store in the refrigerator for 8 to 10 hours. Reheat in the foil at 350 degrees for 40 minutes or until heated through. To serve, spoon some of the warm bell pepper sauce onto each plate and top with 2 slices of the soufflé.

"What really struck me was how fantastic it was just served with slivers of Pecorino."

Chef Ouita Michel

"Woodford has a caramel-y, orange-y, vanilla flavor that goes just great with a seared piece of excellent meat."

Chef Nathan Carlson

Basa with Citrus Reduction

Chef Peng S. Looi, Asiatique and August Moon Chinese Bistro, Louisville, Kentucky

This is a recipe for stretching your culinary wings. The payoff for the effort is a recipe that soars. For an extra dramatic touch, garnish with a dollop of salmon caviar.

4 servings

Basa Fillets
2 tablespoons minced fresh
   lemon grass
2 teaspoons curry powder
2 teaspoons paprika
2 teaspoons Chinese rice wine
2 teaspoons sesame oil
1/2 teaspoon coriander
8 (4-ounce) fresh basa fillets

Asian Fruit Relish
1 mango, chopped
3 kiwifruit, chopped
10 strawberries, chopped
1/4 cup sweet Thai chili sauce
1 tablespoon chopped red onion
1 teaspoon minced Thai holy basil
   or sweet basil

Citrus Reduction
1 mango, chopped
1/2 fresh pineapple, chopped
1/2 cup guava juice
1/2 cup orange juice
1/2 cup grapefruit juice
2 tablespoons sugar
1 to 2 ounces Woodford Reserve
   bourbon
salt and pepper to taste

Sautéed Vegetables and Assembly
1 to 2 tablespoons olive oil
2 teaspoons minced fresh
   gingerroot
1 cup julienned baby bok choy
1 cup julienned red bell pepper
1 cup snow peas, julienned
salt and pepper to taste
1 to 2 tablespoons olive oil

For the basa, mix the lemon grass, curry powder, paprika, wine, sesame oil and coriander in a shallow dish. Add the fillets to the spice mixture and turn until completely coated. Marinate, covered, in the refrigerator for 5 hours, turning occasionally.

For the relish, combine the mango, kiwifruit, strawberries, chili sauce, onion and basil in a bowl and mix well. Chill, covered, for 1 hour. Bring to room temperature before serving.

For the reduction, combine the mango, pineapple, guava juice, orange juice, grapefruit juice and sugar in a saucepan. Cook over medium heat until the mixture is reduced by 20%, stirring frequently. Let stand until cool and process in a blender until puréed. Return the purée to the saucepan and stir in the bourbon. Cook until heated through, stirring frequently. Season to taste with salt and pepper. Remove from the heat and cover to keep warm.

For the vegetables, heat 1 to 2 tablespoons olive oil in a sauté pan until smoke is visible. Stir in the gingerroot. Immediately add the bok choy, bell pepper and snow peas and sauté for 2 to 3 minutes or until tender-crisp. Season to taste with salt and pepper. Remove from the heat and cover to keep warm.

To serve, heat 1 to 2 tablespoons olive oil in a sauté pan until smoke is visible. Sear 2 of the basa fillets in the hot oil for 2 to 3 minutes per side or until crisp, turning once. Remove the fillets to a heated platter to keep warm. Repeat the process with the remaining fillets. Mound 1/4 of the vegetables in the center of each of 4 serving plates and top with 1 basa fillet. Spoon 1 tablespoon of the relish on each fillet and top with the remaining fillets. Spoon additional relish over the fillets and ladle 1/4 cup of the reduction around the fillets and vegetables. Serve immediately.

"I have worked with a number of bourbons, but what amazes me is how well the Woodford plays in a range of recipes, from desserts to very pungent appetizers."

Chef Craig Thompson

"Not only does Woodford add accents, but it takes on other flavors very well. It's not often that you find an ingredient that is both a good giver and receiver of flavors."

Chef Patrick Colley

"And when you get a bourbon that starts with this clear, sweet limestone water of Kentucky–when you start that pure and you triple-distill it–then you end up with such a smooth product, it would be a crime not to use it."

Chef Nat Tate

DESSERTS

Plum Berry Shortcakes

*Chef Mark Williams,
Brown-Forman Corporation,
Louisville, Kentucky*

*Shortcake's not just for kids
anymore, nor is it made for
strawberries alone. The inspired
addition of fresh plums to the
mix makes for a fruit filling
whose dusky richness is
underscored by fine bourbon.*

Makes 10 (2-shortcake) servings

Plum Berry Filling
1 pint fresh strawberries, cut into
  halves
2 cups sliced pitted fresh plums
1/2 cup Woodford Reserve
  bourbon
1/4 cup sugar

Shortcakes and Assembly
33/4 cups flour
1/2 cup sugar
2 tablespoons baking powder
1 teaspoon Woodford Reserve
  bourbon
1/2 teaspoon finely grated orange
  zest
1/8 teaspoon salt
3/4 cup (11/2 sticks) unsalted butter,
  chilled and cut into cubes
11/2 cups heavy cream
2 tablespoons unsalted butter,
  melted
1 tablespoon sugar
1 cup whipping cream
2 tablespoons confectioners'
  sugar
1 tablespoon Woodford Reserve
  bourbon
confectioners' sugar to taste

For the filling, combine the
strawberries, plums, bourbon and
sugar in a bowl and mix gently.
Chill, covered, for 1 hour.

For the shortcakes, sift the flour,
1/2 cup sugar and the baking powder
into a bowl. Stir in 1 teaspoon
bourbon, the orange zest and salt.
Cut the chilled butter into the flour
mixture until crumbly using 2 knives,
a pastry blender or your fingertips.
Add the heavy cream and stir gently
until the mixture adheres. Shape the
dough into a ball. Roll the dough
3/4 inch thick on a lightly floured
surface and cut with a 2-inch cutter.
Arrange the rounds on a baking
sheet and chill for 30 minutes.

Preheat the oven to 400 degrees.
Brush the rounds with the melted
butter and sprinkle with
1 tablespoon sugar. Bake for 17 to
20 minutes or until golden brown.
Let stand until cool.

To serve, combine the whipping
cream, 2 tablespoons confectioners'
sugar and 1 tablespoon bourbon in
a mixing bowl and beat until soft
peaks form, scraping the bowl
occasionally. Cut the shortcakes into
halves and arrange 2 bottom halves
on each of 10 dessert plates. Top
each shortcake half with a dollop of
the whipped cream and a large
spoonful of the filling. Top with the
shortcake tops and sprinkle to taste
with confectioners' sugar.

Chocolate Celebration Cake

Woodford Reserve's kitchen

Makes 1 (10-inch) cake

8 ounces semisweet chocolate,
  coarsely chopped
4 ounces bittersweet chocolate,
  coarsely chopped
11/2 cups (3 sticks) unsalted butter
11/4 cups sugar
3 tablespoons Woodford Reserve
  bourbon
10 egg yolks
10 egg whites
8 ounces pecans, ground
Confectioners' sugar to taste
Caramel Custard Sauce (page 121)

Preheat the oven to 350 degrees.
Grease the bottom and side of a
10-inch springform pan. Line the
bottom with baking parchment
and grease the parchment. Heat
the chocolate in a double boiler
over hot water until blended,
stirring frequently.

Beat the butter and sugar in a
mixing bowl until light and fluffy,
scraping the bowl occasionally. Beat
in the bourbon. Add the egg yolks
1 at a time, beating well after each
addition. Continue beating until the
mixture is smooth. Beat the egg
whites in a mixing bowl until stiff
but not dry peaks form. Fold the
egg whites into the egg yolk mixture
alternately with the chocolate and
pecans. Spoon the batter into the
prepared pan.

Bake for 50 to 55 minutes or until
the center is set. Cool in the pan on
a wire rack for 1 hour and remove
the side. Sprinkle with confectioners'
sugar and slice. Serve with the
Caramel Custard Sauce. You may
prepare up to 1 week in advance
and store, covered, in the refrigerator.

Blackberry Biscuit Pudding

*David Larson, Chef-in-Residence,
Woodford Reserve Distillery,
Versailles, Kentucky*

*When you live in a region where
the biscuit often stands in for
daily bread, the bread pudding
then becomes something
extraordinarily sublime. In fact,
we bet you'll find yourself
making extra biscuits in the
morning just to have this later
the same night.*

10 to 12 servings

The Biscuits
2 cups self-rising flour
11/8 to 11/4 cups heavy cream

The Pudding
6 cups fresh or frozen
  blackberries, lightly mashed
3/4 cup sugar
2 tablespoons flour
grated zest of 1 lemon
3 tablespoons butter, softened
1/3 cup blackberry jam
21/2 cups half-and-half
3/4 cup sugar
6 eggs, beaten
3 tablespoons butter

For the biscuits, preheat the oven to
500 degrees and lightly grease a
baking sheet. Spoon the self-rising
flour into a bowl. Using a fork,
blend in just enough heavy cream
until the dough leaves the side of
the bowl. Gently knead 2 to 3 times
on a lightly floured surface. Roll the
dough 3/4 inch thick and cut into
9 rounds using a 2-inch cutter; do
not twist the cutter. Arrange the
rounds 1 inch apart on a baking
sheet and bake for 5 to 7 minutes
or until golden brown.

For the pudding, combine the
blackberries, 3/4 cup sugar, the flour
and lemon zest in a bowl and mix
well. Let stand for 30 minutes. Split
the biscuits into halves and spread
the cut sides with 3 tablespoons
butter and the jam. Reassemble the
biscuits. Sprinkle a thin layer of the
blackberry mixture over the bottom
of a greased 9×13-inch baking dish.
Arrange the biscuits over the
prepared layer and sprinkle the
remaining blackberry mixture
around the biscuits.

Whisk the half-and-half, 3/4 cup
sugar and the eggs in a bowl until
the sugar dissolves and pour over
the prepared layers, making sure
the biscuit tops are soaked. Chill
for 1 hour. Preheat the oven to
350 degrees. Dot the top with
3 tablespoons butter and place the
baking dish on a baking sheet.
Bake for 40 minutes or until set.
Serve warm with ice cream or
whipped cream.

Cherry Clafouti

*Chef Mark Williams,
Brown-Forman Corporation,
Louisville, Kentucky*

*This clafouti is comfort food
supreme: sweet, warm, and laced
through with the intoxicating
aroma of cherries and Woodford
Reserve. We bet you'll hardly ever
have leftovers.*

6 to 8 servings

2 tablespoons unsalted butter
2 tablespoons brown sugar
1 pound fresh sweet cherries,
  pitted
1/4 to 1/2 cup Woodford Reserve
  bourbon
1/3 cup flour
2 tablespoons cornstarch
1 teaspoon Chinese five-spice
  powder
1/8 teaspoon salt
3/4 cup milk
1/2 cup heavy cream
3 eggs, lightly beaten
1/4 cup sugar
seeds from 1 (2-inch-long) vanilla
  bean, or 1 teaspoon vanilla
  extract
confectioners' sugar to taste

Preheat the oven to 400 degrees.
Coat a shallow 11/2-quart baking
dish with 1 tablespoon of the butter.
Heat the remaining 1 tablespoon
butter and the brown sugar in a
medium sauté pan over medium-
high heat until blended, stirring
frequently. Stir in the cherries and
sauté for 5 minutes or until the
cherries are slightly softened.

Remove from the heat and stir in the
bourbon. Pour the cherry mixture
into the prepared dish.

Mix the flour, cornstarch, five-
spice powder and salt in a bowl.
Whisk the milk, heavy cream, eggs,
sugar and vanilla seeds in a bowl
until combined. Gradually add the
flour mixture to the milk mixture
and stir until incorporated. Spoon
the batter over the prepared layer
and bake for 30 minutes or until set
and beginning to brown around the
edges. Serve warm sprinkled with
confectioners' sugar.

Pineapple Upside-Down Cake

Chef Patrick Colley,
Louisville Country Club,
Louisville, Kentucky

Ripe pineapple and fine bourbon are such a perfect pairing it is a wonder that pineapple is not native to Kentucky. In Patrick Colley's version, Woodford Reserve gives a new perspective to this long-time favorite.

6 to 8 servings

1 cup cake flour
1 teaspoon baking powder
1/8 teaspoon salt
1/2 cup (1 stick) butter, melted
1 cup packed brown sugar
1 (20-ounce) can sliced pineapple, drained
3 egg yolks
1 cup sugar
1/4 cup plus 1 tablespoon Woodford Reserve bourbon
3 egg whites
maraschino cherries, drained and cut into halves (optional)

Preheat the oven to 350 degrees. Sift the flour, baking powder and salt together. Pour the butter into a 9-inch cake pan and stir in the brown sugar until incorporated and moist. Lay enough of the pineapple slices in a single layer over the butter mixture until the bottom of the pan is covered.

Beat the egg yolks and sugar in a mixing bowl at high speed until light and fluffy. Add the flour mixture alternately with the bourbon.

Beat at low speed just until incorporated. Beat the egg whites in a mixing bowl until stiff peaks form. Fold the egg whites into the egg yolk mixture and pour the batter over the pineapple.

Bake for 30 minutes or until a wooden pick inserted in the center comes out slightly moist. Remove from the oven and let stand for 15 minutes. Invert the warm cake onto a serving platter and arrange the cherry halves in the centers of the pineapple slices. Serve warm with whipped cream or ice cream or at room temperature.

White Chocolate Bread Pudding

*Mary Ann Thoren,
Woodford Reserve's kitchen*

White chocolate's subtle, buttery richness is given a whole new dimension with the tawny presence of Woodford Reserve.

6 servings

White Chocolate Sauce
1 cup heavy cream
4 ounces white chocolate, finely chopped
2 tablespoons Woodford Reserve bourbon

Bread Pudding
4 ounces French bread or challah, crusts removed and cut into 1/2 inch cubes
1 1/2 cups half-and-half
1/2 cup heavy cream
4 ounces white chocolate, finely chopped
4 egg yolks
1 egg
1/4 cup sugar
1 1/2 teaspoons vanilla extract

For the sauce, heat the heavy cream in a saucepan over medium heat; do not boil. Add the chocolate and cook until blended, whisking constantly. Remove from the heat and stir in the bourbon. Chill, covered, for up to 1 day.

For the pudding, spread the bread cubes in a single layer on a baking sheet and bake for 10 minutes or until golden brown.

Arrange the bread cubes evenly in 6 lightly greased ramekins or custard cups.

Heat the half-and-half and heavy cream in a saucepan over medium heat. Stir in the chocolate and cook over low heat until blended, stirring constantly. Whisk the egg yolks, egg and sugar in a heatproof bowl until blended. Gradually add 1/4 of the hot cream mixture to the egg mixture, whisking constantly. Whisk in the remaining hot cream mixture until blended and stir in the vanilla. Pour the cream mixture evenly into the prepared ramekins and let stand for 30 minutes or store, covered, in the refrigerator for 8 to 10 hours.

Preheat the oven to 350 degrees. Arrange the ramekins in a 9×13-inch baking pan and add enough boiling water to the baking pan to measure 1 inch. Bake for 25 minutes or just until set. The baking time will have to be lengthened if the ramekins have been chilled.

To serve, reheat the sauce over low heat and drizzle over the warm puddings.

You may bake the bread pudding in a 10-inch round baking dish. Bake without the water bath for 30 to 35 minutes or until set and cut into wedges to serve. You may bake in advance and store, covered, in the refrigerator. Reheat before serving.

Dried Plum Cake

*David Larson, Chef-in-Residence,
Woodford Reserve Distillery,
Versailles, Kentucky*

Winter holidays in the Bluegrass were always marked by the presence of dried fruit and nut cake baked in a bundt pan. Bourbon made their simple goodness richer–and the pleasure only increased when they were served with bourbon-laced eggnog on the side.

12 servings

Cake
1 1/2 cups dried plums, coarsel chopped
3/4 cup Woodford Reserve bourbon
2 cups flour
1 teaspoon cinnamon
1 teaspoon nutmeg
1/2 teaspoon salt
1 cup buttermilk
1 teaspoon baking soda
2 cups sugar
1 cup vegetable oil
3 eggs, lightly beaten
1 1/2 cups pecans, lightly toasted and chopped

Caramel Sauce
1/4 cup (1/2 stick) unsalted butter
1 cup packed light brown sugar
1/2 cup half-and-half

For the cake, soak the plums in the bourbon in a bowl for 30 minutes or for up to 10 hours. Drain, reserving 1 tablespoon of the liquid.

Preheat the oven to 350 degrees. Sift the flour, cinnamon, nutmeg and salt together. Mix the buttermilk and baking soda in a small bowl. Combine the sugar, oil and eggs in a bowl and mix well. Add the flour mixture and buttermilk mixture alternately to the egg mixture, mixing well after each addition. Stir in the reserved liquid, plums and pecans.

Spoon the batter into a buttered and floured bundt or tube pan. Bake for 50 to 60 minutes or until a wooden pick inserted in the center comes out clean. Cool in the pan on a wire rack for approximately 10 minutes and remove the warm cake to a platter.

For the sauce, melt the butter in a saucepan over medium heat. Stir in the brown sugar and cook until blended, stirring frequently. Add the half-and-half and cook over low heat for 5 minutes or until smooth, stirring frequently. Drizzle over the warm cake.

Almond Brittle Torte

*Mary Ann Thoren,
Woodford Reserve's kitchen*

12 servings

The Cake
1 1/2 cups sifted cake flour
3/4 cup sugar
8 egg yolks
3 tablespoons water
2 tablespoons Woodford Reserve
  bourbon
1 teaspoon vanilla extract
8 egg whites
1 teaspoon cream of tartar
1 teaspoon salt
3/4 cup sugar

Almond Brittle and Assembly
1 1/2 cups sugar
1/4 cup light corn syrup
1/4 cup hot water
1/4 teaspoon instant coffee
  granules
1 tablespoon sifted baking soda
3 cups whipping cream
3 tablespoons sugar
2 tablespoons Woodford Reserve
  bourbon
2 cups almond halves or slivers,
  toasted

For the cake, preheat the oven to 350 degrees. Sift the cake flour and 3/4 cup sugar into a bowl. Make a well in the center of the flour mixture and add the egg yolks, water, bourbon and vanilla to the well. Beat until smooth. Beat the egg whites, cream of tartar and salt in a mixing bowl until very soft peaks form. Add 3/4 cup sugar 2 tablespoons at a time and continue beating until a stiff meringue forms. Fold the cake flour mixture into the meringue and spoon into an ungreased 10-inch tube pan. Cut through the batter with a knife, going around the tube 5 or 6 times to break any large air bubbles. Bake for 50 to 55 minutes or until the top springs back when lightly touched. Invert the pan for 1 hour or until cool.

For the brittle, combine 1 1/2 cups sugar, the corn syrup, hot water and coffee granules in a saucepan and mix well. Cook to 300 degrees on a candy thermometer, hard-crack stage. Remove from the heat and imme-diately add the baking soda. Stir vig-orously just until the mixture blends and pulls from the side of the pan.

Immediately pour the foamy mixture into an ungreased shallow 9×9-inch pan; do not spread or stir the mixture. Let stand until cool. Remove the brittle from the pan using a meat mallet or similar tool and place the brittle in a sealable plastic bag. Crush into coarse crumbs using a rolling pin.

To serve, cut the cooled cake crosswise into 4 equal layers. Beat the whipping cream in a mixing bowl until soft peaks form. Fold in 3 tablespoons sugar and the bourbon and spread the whipped cream mixture between the layers and over the top and side of the cake. Gently press the crushed brittle over the top and side of the cake and insert the almonds into the top and side of the cake. Store, covered, in the refrigerator.

Nutty Chocolate Brownies

David Larson, Chef-in-Residence, Woodford Reserve Distillery, Versailles, Kentucky

The ultimate childhood treat takes on a decidedly grown-up twist with the addition of espresso, bourbon, and a pinch of black pepper for bite. Sure, you can still have them warm with milk, but we suggest you try them at least once with Woodford Reserve to sip on the side. Now that's something!

Makes 3 dozen brownies

1 cup (2 sticks) unsalted butter
8 ounces unsweetened chocolate, finely chopped
33/4 cups sugar
5 eggs
21/2 tablespoons instant espresso powder
2 tablespoons Woodford Reserve bourbon
1 tablespoon vanilla extract
1 teaspoon almond extract
1/4 teaspoon salt
1/4 teaspoon pepper
12/3 cups flour
2 cups pecans, toasted and chopped

Preheat the oven to 375 degrees. Coat a 9×13-inch baking pan with butter and line the bottom with baking parchment. Brush the parchment with butter. Heat 1 cup butter and the chocolate in a saucepan over low heat until blended, stirring occasionally.

Combine the sugar, eggs, espresso powder, bourbon, flavorings, salt and pepper in a mixing bowl. Beat at high speed for 10 minutes, scraping the bowl occasionally. Add the chocolate mixture and beat at low speed just until blended. Add the flour and beat at low speed just until combined. Stir in the pecans.

Spread the batter in the prepared pan and smooth the top. Bake for 30 minutes or just until done in the center. Cool to room temperature and invert onto a platter. Let stand for 6 to 10 hours before cutting. Trim off the hard edges and cut into 36 squares.

Race Day Pie

Chef Mark Williams, Brown-Forman Corporation, Louisville, Kentucky

A pie by many names, this Louisville classic is especially prized by fanciers of thoroughbred desserts. We make our version with a crust using the Scottish Shortbread recipe. Whatever you call it, be sure to serve warm, topped with a big scoop of ice cream.

10 servings

Scottish Shortbread*
11/2 cups flour
1/2 cup confectioners' sugar
1/8 teaspoon salt
3/4 cup (11/2 sticks) butter, cut into 1/4-inch cubes and softened
1 egg yolk, beaten
2 tablespoons water
1 teaspoon vanilla extract

Pie Filling
3/4 cup semisweet chocolate chips
3/4 cup pecans, lightly toasted and chopped
1/2 cup sugar
1/2 cup light corn syrup
1/4 cup Woodford Reserve bourbon
1/4 cup (1/2 stick) butter, melted and cooled
1/4 cup flour
3 eggs, lightly beaten
1 teaspoon vanilla extract

For the shortbread, sift the flour, confectioners' sugar and salt into the bowl of a food processor. Add the butter and egg yolk and pulse about 15 times or until crumbly.

Add the water and vanilla and pulse 10 times or just until the mixture adheres. If the dough is sticky, add a couple of tablespoons of flour and pulse 1 or 2 times until combined. Wrap the dough in plastic wrap and chill for 1 hour. The dough may be prepared in advance and stored, covered, in the refrigerator.

For the pie, roll the shortbread dough on a lightly floured surface and pat over the bottom and up the side of a 10-inch pie plate. Chill for 1 hour or longer.

Preheat the oven to 350 degrees. Sprinkle the chocolate chips and pecans over the prepared layer. Mix the sugar, corn syrup, bourbon, butter, flour, eggs and vanilla in a bowl and pour over the chocolate chips and pecans. Bake for 25 to 30 minutes or until the pie jiggles slightly in the center. Let stand for 15 minutes before serving. You may serve later, reheating before serving.

*Labrot and Graham (now the Woodford Reserve Distillery) was where James Crow of Edinborough, Scotland, perfected the art of distilling bourbon. This shortbread recipe will remind you of the imported cookie. The dough is excellent rolled out and cut into desired shapes for cookies, adding 1 teaspoon grated orange or lemon zest to the ingredients.

Fried Green Apples Foster

Chef Mark Williams, Brown-Forman Corporation, Louisville, Kentucky

Fried apples can grace Kentucky tables at any time of the day–perfect for breakfast, lunch, or dinner. This version takes the whole concept uptown for a fantastic flaming finish to tantalize.

2 servings

Bourbon Caramel Sauce
1 1/2 cups sugar
1/4 cup water
1 1/2 teaspoons fresh lemon juice
1 cup heavy cream
2 tablespoons unsalted butter
1/4 cup Woodford Reserve bourbon

Bourbon Caramel Ice Cream
1 quart milk
2 cups sugar
1 vanilla bean, cut lengthwise into halves
6 egg yolks, beaten*
1 tablespoon vanilla extract
2 cups whipping cream, whipped
Fried Green Apples Foster
1/3 cup raisins
2 tablespoons Woodford Reserve bourbon
1/4 cup (1/2 stick) unsalted butter
2 Granny Smith apples, peeled and sliced
juice of 1/2 lemon
1 teaspoon grated lemon zest
6 tablespoons brown sugar
1/4 cup chopped walnuts
1/4 teaspoon cinnamon
1/4 cup Woodford Reserve bourbon
1 teaspoon vanilla extract

For the sauce, combine the sugar, water and lemon juice in a medium heavy saucepan and mix well. Cook over low heat until the sugar dissolves, stirring frequently. Increase the heat to high and bring the syrup to a boil. Boil for 7 minutes or until deep amber in color; do not stir. Remove from the heat and stir in the heavy cream; the mixture will bubble vigorously.

Cook over low heat until any bits of the caramel dissolve, stirring frequently. Whisk in the butter until blended. Remove from the heat and stir in the bourbon. This makes 3 cups.

For the ice cream, heat the milk in a saucepan just to the boiling point. Remove from the heat and add the sugar and vanilla bean, stirring until the sugar dissolves. Cool slightly and stir in the egg yolks. Scrape the brown pulp from the inside of the vanilla bean into the milk mixture and discard the vanilla bean. Stir in the vanilla extract and whipped cream. Cool the milk mixture rapidly and pour into an ice cream freezer container. Freeze using the manufacturer's directions. Mix 2 cups of the Bourbon Caramel Sauce with the ice cream while scraping the ice cream into freezer containers. Freeze for 8 to 10 hours. This makes 2 quarts.

For the fried green apples, soak the raisins in 2 tablespoons bourbon in a bowl for 30 to 60 minutes. Heat the butter in a large sauté pan over medium-high heat and add the apples and lemon juice. Cook for 5 minutes, stirring occasionally.

Drain the raisins and add along with the lemon zest, brown sugar, walnuts and cinnamon to the apple mixture and mix well. Bring to a simmer and remove from the heat. Stir in 1/4 cup bourbon and the vanilla. Ignite the mixture using a long-handled lighter and allow the flames to subside.

To serve, spoon 1 cup of the ice cream into each of 2 dessert bowls and top evenly with the warm apple mixture. You may substitute commercially prepared ice cream for the Bourbon Caramel Ice Cream.

*If you are concerned about using raw egg yolks, use eggs pasteurized in their shells, which are sold at some specialty food stores, or use an equivalent amount of pasteurized egg substitute.

Limestone Truffles

Culinary Director/Owner Jim Gerhardt, Limestone Restaurant, Louisville, Kentucky

Makes 30 to 36 truffles

1 cup heavy cream
1 cup (2 sticks) unsalted butter
1 pound dark semisweet chocolate, finely chopped
1/4 to 1/2 cup Woodford Reserve bourbon
confectioners' sugar

Combine the heavy cream and butter in a saucepan and cook over medium heat until a candy thermometer registers 190 degrees. Remove from the heat and pour over the chocolate in a heatproof bowl. Let stand for 3 minutes and stir until blended. Chill, covered, for 4 to 10 hours.

Scoop the chocolate mixture into small balls and coat with confectioners' sugar. Chill, covered, in the refrigerator.

Baked Pineapple

*David Larson, Chef-in-Residence,
Woodford Reserve Distillery,
Versailles, Kentucky*

*The spicy undertones of
Woodford Reserve and the
straight-up zap of black pepper
turn this dessert fruit into a
seductive side dish.*

8 servings

1 fresh pineapple
1/4 cup packed brown sugar
1/4 cup Woodford Reserve bourbon
2 tablespoons butter, melted
**1 teaspoon coarsely ground
   pepper**

Preheat the oven to 325 degrees.
Core the pineapple and cut into
1/2 to 3/4-inch slices. Cut each slice
into 4 wedges. Overlap the
pineapple wedges on a baking sheet
and sprinkle with the brown sugar.
Drizzle with the bourbon and butter
and sprinkle with the pepper.
Bake for 20 minutes. Broil for 3 to
5 minutes or until light brown.

Caramel Custard Sauce

*Chef Mark Williams,
Brown-Forman Corporation,
Louisville, Kentucky*

*This sauce is delicious drizzled
over fresh fruit.*

Makes approximately 5 cups

22/3 cups half-and-half
3/4 cup packed brown sugar
6 egg yolks
3 tablespoons flour
11/2 teaspoons vanilla extract
1 cup whipping cream, chilled
**3 tablespoons Woodford Reserve
   bourbon**

Scald the half-and-half in a medium
saucepan. Whisk the brown
sugar, egg yolks and flour in a
double boiler until blended. Add
the hot half-and-half gradually,
whisking constantly.

   Cook over boiling water until
thickened, stirring constantly. Set
the top of the double boiler over ice
and let stand until chilled, stirring
occasionally. Stir in the vanilla.

   Beat the whipping cream in a
mixing bowl until stiff peaks form
and blend in the bourbon. Fold the
whipped cream mixture into the
chilled custard and chill, covered,
in the refrigerator.

Chocolate Sauce

*Chef Mark Williams,
Brown-Forman Corporation,
Louisville, Kentucky*

Makes 11/2 cups

7 ounces bittersweet chocolate
2/3 cup milk
2 tablespoons heavy cream
2 tablespoons sugar
**2 tablespoons Woodford Reserve
   bourbon**
2 tablespoons butter, cubed

Heat the chocolate in a double
boiler over simmering water until
melted. Combine the milk, heavy
cream and sugar in a saucepan
and mix well. Cook over high heat
until the mixture comes to a boil,
stirring constantly with a wooden
spoon. Add the hot milk mixture
to the chocolate and stir until
smooth. Bring to a boil and boil
for 15 seconds.

   Remove from the heat and stir in
the bourbon. Add the butter
gradually, mixing until smooth after
each addition. Strain the sauce into a
small pitcher and drizzle over your
favorite dessert. You may store,
covered, in the refrigerator until
needed, reheating before serving.

Capriole Dairy produces some of the finest goat's milk cheese in America. Situated in southern Indiana, just across the Ohio River from Louisville, Kentucky, it's natural that Judy Schad, the dairy's owner and cheese muse, would have been curious about the blend of bourbon and cheese. First came Capriole's award-winning Banon, a lemony, light cheese whose subtleties are brought out dramatically when wrapped in chestnut leaves that have been soaked in bourbon.

"The bourbon releases the tannin in the leaves, and that provides a distinctive harmony note for the cheese that is surprisingly rich," Judy explains. "It was only natural to pair bourbon as a beverage with Banon, then, and not so surprisingly, it only made the flavor of the cheese all the more delightful."

From this first successful marriage, Judy has discovered a number of delicious pairings. A post-supper cheese plate with Woodford Reserve has become one of her favorite dessert courses, and she's developed some guidelines for creating the perfect selection.

Although Banon is a relatively light cheese, Judy has discovered that the best pairings with bourbon happen with what she refers to as "big" cheese. "As a rule, you want a cheese that has a strong flavor of its own, to stand up with the drink, she advises" Mount St. Francis is another Capriole cheese that works well with bourbon. "It's a washed rind cheese with a flavor that's beefy and, well, stinky. It takes a powerful beverage to pair with it and bourbon is so much better than anything else you might think of. The curious thing is, this cheese also has a sweetness to it, and the bourbon brings this out while the cheese works to accent the caramel and nutty tones of the drink."

Likewise a very old Cheddar will work superbly with bourbon, Judy says. "I like a three-year-old Grafton from Vermont, for instance, or an aged farmstead Cheddar from England. They work in the same way that a really great Reggiano will. These are big cheeses with a sweetness, but also a salty taste that links them on the tongue with the bourbon."

Sweetness is what you look for in a blue cheese that will be compatible, avoiding those that are too salty. "There is nothing so wonderful as a fabulous Stilton and a glass of Woodford on the side. I know that people usually think of port with Stilton, but Woodford Reserve has so much more complexity. It's caramelly and smokey; it's got everything a port has going for it but it's not cloying or medicinal."

Fine bourbon also blends well with the "go-withs" that would round out such a cheese plate. "Nuts, of course, are perfect with bourbon; but I also love dried figs and dates. They have a rounded, dark sweetness that the bourbon accents beautifully. You can serve them as they are, or in a cake. I especially like a Spanish fig cake we've discovered that has anise and other spices in it. Fruits that are rich and lend themselves to spiciness are best with bourbon. What you don't want is something too tart, like strawberries in balsamic."

And, of course, Judy points out that not all bourbons are created equal when paired with cheese. "This won't work with a harsh bourbon, one with a sharp, pointed taste. You want a bourbon that had been aged well and has an underlying sweetness. Woodford is perfect in that its edges are all nice and around; fulsome on the tongue. And it's complex, just like a great cheese. It keeps opening up, just like a really good book, which is perhaps the other ingredient you need to make this a perfect evening repast."

INDEX

ACKNOWLEDGMENTS

Cecelia Callahan

Kentucky Chefs

Penny Dant

Dan Dry

Jamie Estes

Julius Friedman

Tim Holz

David Larson

Ronni Lundy

Chris Morris

Linda Nee

Wayne Rose

Mary Ann Thoren

Kentucky Producers:

Bill Best

Blue Moon Garlic

John Medley

Judy Schad

Philip Weisenberger

WOODFORD RESERVE is a registered trademark

Published by Brown-Forman Corporation
Copyright 2005

All rights reserved

This book or any portion hereof may not be
reproduced in any form or by any means,
without written permission of Brown-Forman
Corporation. Any inquiries should be made to
Brown-Forman Corporation, P.O. Box 1080,
Louisville, Kentucky 40201-1080.

ISBN 0 - 9765053 - 0 - 4

Send us your favorite Woodford Reserve recipes.
We would love to hear from you!

For more information about Woodford Reserve
Please contact us at:
The Woodford Reserve Distillery
7855 McCracken Pike
Versailles, Kentucky 40383
Phone: 859-8791812
www.woodfordreserve.com

Written by: Peggy Stevens & Ronni Lundy
Concept and Design: Images, Julius Friedman
Photography: Dan Dry, Julius Friedman,
& ChrisWitzeke
Test Kitchen: Mary Ann Thoren & Linda Nee
Food Stylist: Julius Friedman
Printing: Hamilton Printing
Editing and Distribution: FRP